KINGDOM Life

God's Original Intent for Christianity

LUTHER ARMSTRONG

CITI OF
BOOKS

CITIOFBOOKS, INC.
3736 Eubank NE Suite A1
Albuquerque, NM 87111-3579
www.citiofbooks.com
Hotline: 1 (877) 389-2759
Fax: 1 (505) 930-7244

Ordering Information:
Quantity sales. Special discounts are available on quantity purchases by corporations, associations, and others. For details, contact the publisher at the address above.

Printed in the United States of America.

ISBN-13:   Softcover   979-8-89391-789-5
               eBook   979-8-89391-790-1

Library of Congress Control Number: 2025913779

TABLE OF CONTENTS

KINGDOM LIFE

Making you the fullness of the measure and stature of Christ
Conforming you to His Image

Unless otherwise indicated, all scripture are quoted from the King James or New King James and English Standard Versions of the Bible.

Second Edition Page

This second edition of Kingdom Life was prompted by several revelations given after the publishing of my first edition. I felt it important to settle the primary question of Jesus Kingdom being established now and not after we die. This question was not properly addressed in my first book, so I have addressed this fully in this edition.

Secondly, I have revealed that two Covenants not one Covenant was made when Jesus hung and died on the cross of Calvary. This was not just another event, but The Event of Man Kind's existence which gave us equal authority with God to take control of the earth as God's family and Heirs of this earth defacto. We don't just live here, we are co-owners of Jesus Kingdom because of our faith. We are obligated to carry out the Will of God so His Kingdom is build the way He desires. This relationship makes us co-equal to Christ and this is why the devil seeks Christians to come under his influence and humanity by default.

I pray you gain revelation of your full authority as a believer and member of God's family in today's world of demonic infestation.

PREFACE

If you are looking for more of Jesus and are willing to get out of the box of religion to do it, Kingdom Life offers a path for you. These new concepts will challenge you to set your sights on things above in a way that requires you to mentally adjust to the Spirit of God. We call this having the "Mind of Christ" (1 Cor 2:16). However, this mind allows us according to 1 Corinthians 2:9 to refocus and enjoy "…what no eye has seen, no ear has heard, and no human mind has conceived these are the things God has prepared for those who love him". (NIV)

As you begin to pursue these options you will begin to understand Kingdom Life. Kingdom Life is a higher calling than you have ever experienced.

We as the Body of Christ have limited God's ability to what we have experienced or what we have not experienced. God has not been able to break through these blockages to elevate our minds to embrace the new and bold things of God. Our Lord has so much more for us according to the above scripture. God's heart breaks that our faith is so low, yet we declare our faith is so high!

We must embrace a mind shift that will have the world wondering where these Christians have gotten these new abilities and demonstrations of boldness. God made you for this very thing; to demonstrate His Glory to the world (Jn 17:all). You don't have to dream about doing what Jesus did, you can do what Jesus has done and more when you have shifted into Kingdom Thinking. Kingdom Life will then shift you out of the material world into the world of the "… perfect man, unto the measure of the stature of the fullness of Christ." (Eph 4:13) The things that others have said cannot be done will be done through you as you develop Kingdom Life in Christ.

Ps 103:7 says, "[7] He (God) made known his ways unto Moses, his acts unto the children of Israel." If you are willing to learn God's <u>ways</u> by receiving specific impartations that empower you to know how God accomplishes the things he does, God will activate you like he did Moses, God will reveal how and why and what HE has created in the universe. How could Moses have gone back and written the Book of Genesis about God's beginning creation without being given detailed explanation of the exact process. Indeed God took Moses into heaven itself and showed him the tabernacle so that Moses could duplicate that architecture on earth.

Exodus 26:30 tells us this is how God trained Moses; "And thou shalt rear up the tabernacle according to the fashion thereof which was shewed thee in the mount." In contrast to understanding the original plans of God as Moses did, most Christians are satisfied with having one problem eliminated by getting a miracle or a healing, or some other action. His acts would be sufficient for us with this frame of mind (the miracles, signs, and wonders). Most people are simply too busy to appreciate and learn the skills Jesus displayed by the Spirit or learn the knowledge from Jesus' mind in order to be transformed into his exact image. I caution you not to look for some science fiction image or experience. We must avoid counterfeits of Jesus' power while pressing into the Mind of Christ and allow Jesus to teach us what blocks us from learning. Revelations 13: 11-13 tells us of a beast who will do great signs like calling down fire from heaven while people are watching. This is similar to Elijah's calling down fire to destroy his enemies in 2 Kings 1:10,14. Don't be fooled by the devil's counterfeit actions. Jesus will know you because you like him.

1 John 3:1-7 states, " Behold, what manner of love the Father hath bestowed upon us, that we should be called the sons of God: therefore the world knoweth us not, because it knew him not.² Beloved, now are we the sons of God, and it doth not yet appear what we shall be: but we know that, when he shall appear, we shall be like him; for we shall see him as he is. ³And every man that hath this hope in him purifieth himself, even as he is pure. ⁴Whosoever committeth sin transgresseth also the law: for sin is the transgression of the law. ⁵And ye know that he was manifested to take away our sins; and in him is no sin. ⁶Whosoever abideth in him sinneth not: whosoever sinneth hath not seen him, neither known him. ⁷Little children, let no man deceive you: he that doeth righteousness is righteous, even as he is righteous." (KJV)

God's actions are to protect and defend you from the works of the devil, not trick you into violating His commands and way of life. I believe the popular television and movie series "Star Trek" depicts the idea that the universe is a multi-faceted architectural expanse where differing ecological planets exist without disturbing the next geographic model of life. God willingly showed Moses on Mt. Sinai that He had created no such diversity or geography in His universe. Only the human race was included in God's creation and therefore you are a candidate to learn and experience the same things Moses experienced. You can be shown the beginning of the universe and life through Jesus Kingdom.

Kingdom Life is for you!

INTRODUCTION

Kingdom Life, which begins with salvation, starts a series of transactions in our individual lives that activate the first stages of metamorphosis allowing us to enter Jesus Kingdom. These events are similar to what happened to Jesus when he was baptized by John the Baptist. These events would direct his future from that day forward. The Holy Spirit would lead Jesus into the wilderness to be alone and figure out the changes that happened to him after being baptized. Jesus felt the presence of God in a way He never felt before in his humanity. What did these changes mean for his future. Jesus found himself in a firestorm of conflict and danger he was not prepared for. Fortunately, the 40 day fast he had just completed became a life-saving event. A destiny was activated for Jesus that was both violent and miraculous at the same time. Jesus didn't know this was coming. He just went to take a swim with his cousin down at the river and found himself in a fight that would almost take his life. Jesus stepped through a portal in the Spirit realm that revealed what he was called to accomplish and that portal redirected every step he would take from that day forward.

Let's review the events. Jesus goes down to the Jordan river where his cousin, John the Baptist, was designated to transition every person who came to his ceremony under the influence of the Holy Spirit. John was just following orders. He didn't know who this anointing was for. All he knew was that when he saw the "Dove of God" come down, that was the man God picked for himself. The process of transition begins when you receive salvation. Each individual saint starts the road to compliance and alignment with God's plan so we can become the exact image and likeness of Christ himself. Embracing this truth activates one of the two full-time purposes for every Christian's life. Achieving this goal allows God to influence the entirety of each human life to do His will every day. God is transferring His Kingdom to the earth through you. You become His anointed vessel so His Kingdom will come and His will is being done on earth as it is in heaven (Mt 6:9-13). Man is expected to exhibit all of the characteristics of Christ. By doing this we become easily recognizable as Christians to the world.

Jesus came preaching <u>the Kingdom of God and His righteousness</u> as the standard for living a Godly life on earth. Every disciple understood this truth because the kingdom message was the most preached message that Jesus talked about. The single most important and sought after ability was how to live in the Kingdom. Kingdom conversations were the most discussed and debated subject. Almost all questions referenced the coming Kingdom. Even after the resurrection, the disciples would want to know when this Kingdom would come.

Acts 1:4-8... ⁴ And being assembled together with *them*, He commanded them not to depart from Jerusalem, but to wait for the Promise of the Father, "which," He said, "you have heard from Me; ⁵ for John truly baptized with water, but you shall be baptized with the Holy Spirit not many days from now." ⁶ Therefore, when they had come together, they asked Him, saying, "Lord, will You at this time restore the kingdom to Israel?" ⁷ And He said to them, "It is not for you to know times or seasons which the Father has put in His own authority. ⁸ But you shall receive power when the Holy Spirit has come upon you; and you shall be [c]witnesses to Me in Jerusalem, and in all Judea and Samaria, and to the end of the earth."

You notice that after Jesus had ascended into the sky, "The Kingdom Came." The Kingdom was no longer waiting in the hands of the Father, The Kingdom had come through Jesus physical resurrection. The disciples not only received the Holy Spirit, they received the 2nd wave of the Kingdom. Jesus said that if I don't go, the Power of the Kingdom would not come. Jesus went away and received His Kingdom and returned to establish that Kingdom through His Ekklesia…the church, his governing body. We were given co-equal authority to manage our part of His church. What Jesus had just declared as "only in the hands of the Father," was now known by every disciple. They had the "Power to demonstrate God's presence!" Every believer had the authority to "Spread the power of the Kingdom to every person they met." No Titles were needed. The Kingdom is HERE!

Mark 16:17-20 gives the key elements of Kingdom Life. In Jesus name, preach the gospel, baptize in Jesus' name, cast out demons, speak with new tongues, take up serpents and if you drink deadly things you will not be harmed, lay hands on the sick and they shall recover. If you aren't doing this, begin so you can start living Kingdom Life. Kingdom Life is identified by the demonstration of God's power in your life. The Kingdom was always on the lips and hearts of Jesus and the disciples. Achieving the goal of Kingdom Life was the single most important goal of Jesus Ministry. In the name of Jesus the disciples cast out devils, healed the sick, raised the dead, and received provision to serve that purpose. So must we.

Jesus shared this subject more than any other according to Mt 6:33 in contrast to the messages we hear today. Every disciple knew what the Kingdom represented and was eager to learn how to inter-act with what Jesus said was the biggest thing since creation. Citizens of the Kingdom will have a lifestyle focused on "every word that proceeds from the mouth of the father. Kingdom Life is centered around "Every Word coming out of the mouth of the Father." (Mt 4:4) Jesus taught a new way of living as well as a new way of thinking. Every man and woman was expected to adopt as their own the habits that made Kingdom matters the most important matter of the day. Jesus said, "I am the way, the truth and the life" and He groomed each man to live the Kingdom way. As such, Kingdom Life, not earth life will require all your attention.

Kingdom Life is not Earth Life.
Kingdom Life is not Human Life.
Kingdom Life is not Church Life.
Kingdom Life is not Tribal or Social or Cultural Life.
Kingdom Life is not American Life.

CHAPTER 1

KINGDOM LIFE

Matthew 6:33

Life in Jesus' Kingdom is somewhat mystical from the viewpoint of most Christians. I don't think this concept was mystical during Jesus' day, but accepted as the fulfillment of God's covenant promise. Jesus presented these concepts as opposing views to the status quo of the Pharisees and Sadducees who were the spiritual leaders of the day and made this revelation the primary focus of his message while on earth. Even after Jesus' resurrection and imminent departure from earth to heaven, the apostle's focus was still on The Kingdom. We hear the question in Acts 1:6 from the Apostles asking Jesus," …Lord, will you now restore The Kingdom to Israel."

In this time of great challenge to the Church our primary tenets of faith need refreshing. Every person following Jesus in that day knew that The Kingdom was the subject to which Jesus gave his full focus and direction in ministry. Jesus used Kingdom teaching exclusively to impart and give vision to each one of His followers. Jesus said nothing that did not pertain to The Kingdom.

<u>Matthew 4:23</u>

And Jesus went about all Galilee, teaching in their synagogues, and preaching the gospel of the kingdom, and healing all manner of sickness and all manner of disease among the people.

Kingdom Life is The Life of God living in you, the fullness of the measure and stature of Jesus Christ conforming you to HIS image.

Let's talk about Jesus conversation with Pilate in John 18:33-38

Jesus is standing before Pilate, the Roman Governor of Judea who was the ruler in Jerusalem, the capital city of Israel. The Sanhedrin, a group of Jewish religious leaders who claimed to be the Spiritual Head of the Nation of Israel, has delivered Jesus to Pilate to be killed because Jesus has declared himself "The Son of God". Jesus openly acknowledged that He is God's Son and that He will be seen sitting at the right hand of God the Creator. (read Lk 22:66-71) As a result of this statement the Jewish leadership beat Jesus and took him to Pilate, the Roman governor, to be crucified.

Mankind has long established that a dying man's confession is the most truthfully spoken words during his life. Yet Jesus chose this conversation to become the last real conversation he would have before his death.

There is no Kingdom if there is no King and there is no King if there is no Kingdom!

The words you are about to read happened before Jesus was hung on the cross of Calvary.

Timing is everything! So these words of this conversation are Pre – Crucifixion. These words would take on a different meaning after the Resurrection has taken place. Every Word would fulfill the claims made by Jesus before he died.

Jesus is having this conversation with Pilate the Roman Governor... John 18:33-37 (ESV)

33 So Pilate went back into the governor's headquarters, [a] summoned Jesus, and asked him, "Are you the king of the Jews?"

34 Jesus replied, "Are you asking this on your own initiative, or did others tell you about me?"

35 Pilate replied, "I am not a Jew, am I? It is your own nation and high priests who have handed you over to me. What have you done?"

36 Jesus answered, "My kingdom does not belong to this world. If my kingdom belonged to this world, my servants would fight to keep me from being handed over to the Jewish leaders. [b] But for now my kingdom is not from here."

37 Pilate asked him, "So you are a king? Jesus answered, "You say that I am a king. I was born for this, and I came into the world for this: to testify to the truth. Everyone who is committed to the truth listens to my voice."

At the time he spoke these words, at that moment there was no kingdom nor was there a resurrection. On the surface it appeared that Jesus was talking nonsense.

In Matthew 27 verse 50 the word says: 50 And Jesus cried out again with a loud voice, and yielded up His spirit. (51) Then, behold, the veil of the temple was torn in two from top to bottom; and the earth quaked, and the rocks were split, 52 and the graves were opened; and many bodies of the saints who had fallen asleep were raised; 53 and coming out of the graves after His resurrection, they went into the holy city and appeared to many.

The Power of the resurrection created the transformation of the earth into the Kingdom of Jesus Christ

Jesus would fulfil his promise John 2:19which says,"...destroy this temple and in three days I will raise it up."

Revelation 1:18 I am he that liveth, and was dead; and, behold, I am alive for evermore, Amen; and (I) have the keys of hell and of death.

On the surface it appears what Jesus was saying about his kingdom was not true. But after Jesus is resurrected from the dead, the things spoken in Mt 27:50-53 began to happen in broad daylight. "The Kingdom of Jesus Christ is born into the world and the conversation Jesus had with Pilate was NO Longer True! Jesus Kingdom had come to earth as a result of His Resurrection Status! Jesus is ALIVE and HIS Kingdom is alive also!

Upon Jesus death, burial and resurrection the Kingdom would come roaring into life. Jesus' Kingdom is established and thechurch is born and planet earth is given back to man according to Ps 115:16... "the heavens, the heavens belong to God, but the earth he has given to the children of men."

Heb 1:8-13 tells us, "8 But unto the Son he saith, Thy throne, O God, is forever and ever: a scepter of righteousness is the scepter of thy kingdom. 9 Thou hast loved righteousness, and hated iniquity; therefore God, even thy God, hath anointed thee with the oil of gladness above thy fellows. 10 And, Thou, Lord, in the beginning hast laid the foundation of the earth; and the heavens are the works of thine hands: 11 They shall perish; but thou remainest; and they all shall wax old as doth a garment; 12 And as a vesture shalt thou fold them up, and they shall be changed: but thou art the same, and thy years shall not fail. 13 But to which of the angels said he at any time, Sit on my right hand, until I make thine enemies thy footstool."

Jesus being born flesh and blood now establishes the renewed ownership of earth as HIS Kingdom and declares the truth of Mt 6:10 "…thy kingdom come thy will be done on earth as it is in heaven."

CHAPTER 2

"THE KINGDOM IS THE EARTH, BUT NOT EARTH LIFE"

"I am a King and I have my Kingdom..." Lk 22:29-30

Jesus was crowned King of His Kingdom at his birth in Bethlehem so we would not have to be conformed to earth life. Reading St. John chapter 3 there was a conversation going on with a man named Nicodemus who had come to Jesus at night with a question. However, before Nicodemus could ask his question, Jesus said to him, "...you must be born again..." Nicodemus could not comprehend these words, so he said, How can a man be born when he is old? Can he enter a second time into his mother's womb and be born? (NKJV)"

The answer to Nicodemus statement is NO. You cannot go back into your mother's womb and be born physically. But you can be born again spiritually. Since the Spirit of a Man is the life of the body, reestablishing the God Spirit in your body transitions you into God's Kingdom.

Sins associated with the human spirit are eradicated during the New Birth and ALL sin is forgiven during the "Act of Salvation." This means Kingdom Life is NOT earth life. Rom 12:2 states, "Do not be conformed to this world, but be transformed by the renewing of your mind that

6

you will prove what is that good and acceptable and perfect will of God." Kingdom life makes it possible for every believer to accomplish the good, acceptable and perfect will of God without concern about failing the master. The Blood of Jesus has been shed to pay the price for our shortcomings.

Original sin has been eliminated through the blood of Jesus. All self-condemnation or other accusations presented by Satan are destroyed. (Rom 8:1) Satan continues to accuse us for every little mistake we make, even though Jesus declares us righteous. Job had the same problem (Job 1:6-12). These accusations open doors for harassing spirits to enter our life. Jesus Blood destroys ALL sin and all accusing spirits. Jesus redeemed the earth from the curse and bought back everything Adam lost according to Psalms 24. As a result of redemption, I can shout I've been redeemed in the face of the devils plots, schemes and accusations. The actions that took place with Job are not the actions God decreed for us. You can have the God kind of Life (Zoe) as we walk in the footsteps of Christ. Our transition into "The Kingdom of Jesus Christ" produces that supernatural authority and victory Jesus paid to deliver us from death, hell and the grave. (Rev 1:18) God delivered us out of the kingdom of darkness into the Kingdom of his Son (Col 1:13). This transference means everything when it comes to receiving authority to change the circumstances of life.

Mankind is a 3-part being and as a result of being born again, the real you became the same as Christ Jesus. You live in a body, but all of your earthly transactions are processed through your soul which contains your mind, will, and emotions according to 1 Thessalonians 5:23.

"23 Now may the God of peace Himself sanctify[a] you completely; and may your whole spirit, soul, and body be preserved blameless at the coming of our Lord Jesus Christ."

Being born again allows us the ability to function as Dual Citizens because of our family relationship as shared in Gal 4:1-7. We are adopted into the family of God as Joint Heirs. Kingdom Life gives us access right now to the glorious heaven Paul describes in 2 Cor 12:2-4.

TWO THINGS HAPPENED ON THE CROSS OF CALVARY, NOT ONE THING

1. The first is that Jesus made a Blood Covenant with God our Creator, for the soul of every man, woman, boy, and girl. Every Human Person can be saved. This experience is reserved just for humans. No animals are excepted in this category even though there are animals in heaven. These are ccreations of God that do not have the Breath of Life from God.

2. The 2nd Covenant is for those being Born Again (John 3:3) These saints can enter eternal life as the redeemed family of God. This opportunity means, I MUST ask Jesus to be my savior and Lord. This action, allows my sins to be forgiven and make me a new creation and member of God's family

Jesus first Covenant is for you individually and Jesus second Covenant allows God the Father to not destroy the earth before receiving everyone that wants to be saved. Jesus Blood sacrifice destroys ALL SIN.

GOD PUT HIMSELF INSIDE OF YOU

John 14:15-18… the Holy Spirit lives "In You"

John 14:19-20… Jesus the Son lives "In You:

John 14:23…God the Father lives "In You"
Gal 4:1-7…says you are Now an Adopted Son

John 17:14-28…"You are not of this world…"

Your SIN nature is destroyed by the Blood of Jesus You Gain Jesus' Divine Nature Inside of YOU

2 Pt 1:3-4 -

2 Cor 5:17-21-I call this the Divine Exchange

This is what makes the requirements of the Life of God possible. God exchanges Jesus' Divine nature for your Sin Nature. We sometimes call this the Adamic Nature. We also call this place "Original Sin" referring to the sin of Adam. God bestows Jesus Divine Nature upon us, so we can become the Perfect Man the Bible tells us we have to be. This is not by our works, but by the supernatural impartation of God as each believer is transformed by Jesus Blood. 2 Cor 5:17-21 tells us that God the Father made Jesus SIN for us who knew no sin, so that we would be the righteousness of God in Christ Jesus. This makes us DIVINITY!

By accepting this exchange we become HOLY and RIGHTEOUS before God. All the old things are passed away, behold ALL things are become new (vs 17). All all of our spots, blemishes and wrinkles are gone according to Col 1:21-23. Also God presents us as having NO spots, blemishes, or wrinkles as indicated in Eph 5:27. This is compliant with the requirements of Holiness that God set in Heb 12:14. God wipes out every hindrance and restriction according to scripture that would hold us out of His presence. It doesn't matter how you feel, it only matters what God says. Your works are as filthy rages. (Isa 64:6) God gives us his righteousness through Jesus Blood Sacrifice.

During the forty days after his resurrection, Jesus clarified statements he had made concerning his Kingdom. (1) In Mt 16:28 Jesus says, "Verily I say to you, there be some standing here, which shall not taste of death till they see the Son of Man coming in his Kingdom." Here Jesus begins talking about His Kingdom. This happened in Acts 1:1-

8. Jesus Kingdom was activated on Earth during Jesus ascension from earth to heaven. (2) In Mt 20:20-23, the mother of James and John asked a favor of Jesus. "...Grant us that we may sit, one on your right and the other on your left, in your glory..." This also shows that Jesus Kingdom was activated during the 40 days he was on earth.

There are actually <u>3 Godly Kingdoms Revealed</u> in scripture. The kingdoms of this world as stated in Mt. 4:8 are excluded from this revelation.

These kingdoms are excluded from the kingdoms Satan referenced in Mt 4:1-11.

1) According to 1 Cor 15:24-25 we clearly see 2 Kingdoms being exchanged since Jesus is transferring his kingdom to the Father. Godly as verse 24 says"...then cometh the end, when he shall have delivered up the Kingdom to God, even the Father; when he shall have put down all rule and all authority and power." "vs 25 "...For he must reign, till he hath put all enemies under his feet."(Heb 1:13)

2) If Jesus' Kingdom was the same as His Father's Kingdom, there would be no transference of power to take place. Everything would be as it was. So it is clear that we have more than one place called Kingdom

3) One Kingdom is managed by God the other managed by Jesus the Son as He serves the Plan of God. Paul received training for his ministry in both realms. One realm was on earth as stated in Gal 1:15-17 and the other training in the third heaven of 2 Cor 12:1-4 where unspeakable information about God's Kingdom plans were granted for earthly ministry.

The point is that if we wait to utilize our Kingdom authority until after we die, we miss the opportunity to demonstrate the power of Jesus Kingdom Life to change the world. Non-believers are the ones who need to see God demonstrate through us to confirm I need to be saved. As believers we are the ones who are preparing the earth for Jesus' second coming just as John the Baptist prepared the Jews for Jesus' first coming. Jesus' Kingdom is active today and we prove this truth by demonstrating the gifts, talents, and anointings of Isa 11:1-5. This is the way Jesus ministered on earth in his day. We must walk the earth TODAY just like Jesus did and we must demonstrate the same things in order for His mandate to be fulfilled in the earth in our lifetime. Thy kingdom come, thy will be done on earth as it is in heaven..."(Mt 6:10) is still the purpose we believers are here.

As the Church, we must not defer the usage of these tools so that this demonstration makes believers of those who don't know Jesus today. The ideology that these tools and gifts are reserved for heaven is false. God the Father is in Heaven and Nobody and nothing is going to up-stage GOD in heaven. God our Creator is supreme! No miracles, signs, and wonders will be done in Heaven. Therefore, the church (Ekklesia) of the earth is a sub-culture of Kingdom Life. Miracles, signs, and wonders are to be demonstrated on the earth only so that people can recognize there is a heaven to enter. Miracles don't come just because you live on earth. They come because you have Kingdom Life operating in you through Jesus Christ.

Jesus demonstrated this as he went from one location to the other following the Father's directives. Walking on water is a Kingdom activity. Multiplying the loaves and fish is a Kingdom activity. Turning water into wine is a Kingdom activity. Just like the transfiguration on the Mountain of Transfiguration was a Kingdom activity. Jesus did them all while he was in his <u>human body on earth</u>, not in heaven. These acts represent <u>Kingdom Life</u>! Romans 12:2 demands that we be TRANSFORMED in order to properly receive the ability to operate as Jesus did in harmony with The Father. Yet, it is absolutely true that only Christians can do what Jesus did! We must become purposefully intentional now while accepting and embracing the "Mind of Christ." We must no longer depend on our earthly intelligence, but accept "The Mind of Christ" (1 Cor 2:16) so we can walk like, talk like, think like, and act like Jesus did on earth.

Dr. Myles Munroe describes Kingdom Life from the perspective of a government governing mankind. He says this, "Simply stated, the Bible is about a King, a Kingdom, and a royal family of children." He goes on to say, "...the Bible is a story and message about the desire of a King to extend his Kingdom to new territories through his royal family. The Bible, therefore, is about government and governing."

I believe that Dr. Munroe would agree with the statement that Kingdom Life is given to replace all governmental patterns and methods in the earth today. Nothing is to be left out of the current methods except where those concepts agree with the Bible. These methods of governance contaminated by original sin. Every pattern from the earth is rejected in the Kingdom.

Yet it is true that, "government is about order, influence, administration, distribution, protection, maintenance, accountability, responsibility, and productivity." Dr. Munroe also states that, "technically speaking, government is the person, group, or organization that executes the functions of governing." (Kingdom Principles, pg 42, para 3)

Sadly, humanity has adopted a "Star Trek" mentality by thinking that we can upgrade and improve our human status at will to avoid the penalties of sin. Humanity believes that those upgrades will be acceptable and sufficient to fix the problems on earth without God. However, there is no upgrade that can operate in the place of Kingdom Life. The more we look like Jesus, the more things happen like it happened with Jesus. We must begin this journey like Jesus TODAY, not after we die.

Jesus didn't establish Kingdom Life to debate, compare or compete with earth life. Jesus fully intends Kingdom Life to replace earth life to establish and grow <u>His Kingdom</u> on earth as the only way for all people to live.

Many of us have been brought up to repeat the Lord's Prayer before going to sleep at night. RIGHT? Have you really considered the words of that prayer in context to what I am saying? Let's take a look:

Matthew 6:9-13 (KJV)
[9] After this manner therefore pray ye: Our Father which art in heaven, Hallowed be thy name. [10] Thy kingdom come, Thy will be done in earth, as it is in heaven. [11] Give us this day our daily bread. [12] And forgive us our debts, as we forgive our debtors. [13] And lead us not into temptation, but deliver us from evil: For thine is the kingdom, and the power, and the glory, forever. Amen.

<u>There is a difference between God the Father's physical Kingdom</u> which is fixed in heaven and Jesus Kingdom designed for our Glorified Bodies. The Father's Kingdom does not move while Jesus' Kingdom is fully transferrable to earth from the Spirit Realm at the appropriate time. Revelations 21:1-7 shows that God the Father's Kingdom remains in heaven while at the same time Jesus is fulfilling His Kingdom call on earth. This completes another promise God the Father made to Jesus that He must rule "until his enemies are made his footstool" (Isa 66:1). The Bible is clear that Jesus will return a third time and begin to rule the earth from Jerusalem for 1000 years. This promise does not mean that Jesus does nothing until His enemies are made His foot stool. Jesus will destroy His enemies and rule over them as stated in Rev 19: 11- 21 and Rev 20:1-7. Most Christians call this <u>the Millennial Reign</u> of Christ.

Jesus' statement to Pilate that "my kingdom is not of this world" was not talking about His Kingdom not residing on earth. Jesus only stated that His Kingdom was not on earth now. Soon Jesus would die on the Cross of Calvary and His resurrection would bring His Kingdom to Life as Abraham and the patriarchs rose from the grave. This happened in Mt 27:50-53. This is when Jesus Kingdom was established on earth.

Now we wait for Jesus Kingdom rule on earth which will begin Jesus third visitation to earth. Last of all, <u>God the Father</u> will merge these Kingdoms to replace the earth forever. (Rev 21)

TWO different Kingdoms established in the same place. But until then, we must "...Seek first the Kingdom..." (Mt 6:33) Jesus intends us to focus primarily on establishing His Kingdom on earth as his ambassadors' or as "Kingdom Managers" and servants. Today we have this management responsibility as we spread the Gospel to every nation making disciples.

TRANSFORMATION AND METAMORPHOSIS

Rom 12:2-3

At the time of salvation we automatically enter the Transformation process, but when you enter the process of Metamorphosis you enter Kingdom Life.

<u>1 Corinthians 15:24:</u>

Then cometh the end, when he shall have delivered up the (Jesus) kingdom to God (the Creator), even the Father; when "...he shall have put down all rule and all authority and power ...", against His (Jesus) Kingdom.

These words also coincide with the words of God the Father in;

Heb 1: 13 "... But to which of the angels said he at any time, Sit on my right hand, until I make thine enemies thy footstool?"... (Ps 110:1)

Obviously God the Father had Jesus' Kingdom on His mind when he wrote these verses of scripture.

Even though we enter Kingdom Life at the time of salvation, we do not LIVE Kingdom Life until we are "actively in the Process of Metamorphosis.."

How does that happen? We must begin to operate the gifts of the Spirit. You don't have to heal everybody, but you do have to try and believe these things are possible for you!

The greater one is in you (1 John 4:4). Kingdom Life produces in your spirit the Spirit of Jesus, just like Jesus was on the earth. The only difference is that your blood can not forgive sins.

We must examine ourselves in all areas of the Kingdom to become fully proficient in the Life of the Kingdom. Kingdom Life declares itself by how we live as Kingdom citizens. Our demonstration of Kingdom Life is the declaration that "Kingdom Life lives in ME". The more we begin to look Just Like Jesus, the more Kingdom Life is expressed in us. Man looks on the outward parts, but God looks on the heart (1 Sam 16:7). Tremendous activity happens when you look like Jesus. Those activities won't happen when you don't look like Jesus. When your ways please the Lord, He will make your enemies be at peace with you. (Pro 16:7)

We must watch the Spiritual markers that identify who we are and what we stand for. We must begin to Operate the Gifts of the Spirit as described in 1 Cor 12:4-9, Eph 4:11-13, Rom 12:3-9, Mk 16:17-20 and Gal 4:1-8. We must become intentionally purposeful in accomplishing the transformation necessary to complete "the fullness of the measure and stature of Christ". (Eph 4:13) Only then will we see this process being completed. Expect Transformation (change), expect to become just like Jesus as stated in the book of Romans. Rom 12:2(NKJV) which says, " ...and do not be conformed to this world, but be transformed by the renewing of your mind so you can prove what is that good and acceptable and perfect will of God...". Only then will you activate Kingdom Life in and around you, for it is Your expectation that causes Metamorphosis to happen.

Earth life can only produce darkness (Gen 1:2) "In the beginning the earth was without form and void; and darkness was upon the face of the deep…" Kingdom Life is a life of VALUE and LIGHT. You are the beloved of the Lord. Animals, fish, even the earth do not take priority over our human relationship with God our Creator.

According to the book of Genesis, everything made was to be used for the existence of mankind (Gen 9:1-7). Nothing on earth is more valuable than mankind. What a stark contrast to the mindset of today's social structure. Today's cry is to save everything but the human element. That mindset has led to world destruction through drugs, alcohol, human trafficking, war, starvation, and hate because man has determined the value of a soul rather than God.

Kingdom Life requires that earthly ways be eliminated in us in order for Kingdom Life to become dominant. (John 3:3) We are entering a new decade causing Kingdom Life to come to a dominant position in the world. We are the preparers of Jesus' return. There has been a shift in power to the saints as stated in Daniel 7:22 causing us to dominate the atmosphere. This is why evil will be seen as evil and the light of Jesus Christ will shine as the morning star.

Earth life can only produce darkness. Human life can only produce SIN after Adam sold out to Satan. "Therefore death came to ALL mankind" (Rom 5:13; 16:8-9) and man has been trying to produce life every since in the natural. Consequently, the organized Church's embrace of earthly operating methods is the source of the loss of power and authority which serves to divide Christ's Body and prevent by doctrine the miracle opportunities of Christ. We are supposed to be unifying the world around the concepts of The Kingdom and thereby making the world The Kingdom of Jesus Christ according to the Lord's Prayer (Mt 6:9-15). Instead we have only divided the world based on our individual beliefs. Where is Jesus' Kingdom in that? (Rom 5:12-21)

Kingdom Life is the true way for us to live. There is no God like Jehovah. "Jesus is the way, the truth, and the LIFE". "No man comes to the Father except through the Son…" And Jesus is the King of His Kingdom. "So let's make it so."

KINGDOM LIFE REMOVES ANY DISPUTE THAT SATAN OWNS THE EARTH.
KINGDOM LIFE RETURNS EARTH OWNERSHIP TO GOD LIKE BEFORE ADAM.
THEREFORE ALL KINGDOM FUNCTIONS ARE TO CHANGE THE EARTH INTO GOD'S WAY OF LIVING

Kingdom Life transitions us from FOCUSING ON SIN to focusing on Jesus' Life as the example. Living an earthly life keeps us focused on SIN and OURSELVES in everything. In The Kingdom, sin is not a factor (1 Jn 1:9). Why is sin not a factor? Because Jesus has taken care of ALL SIN. How much SIN has Jesus' Blood destroyed? ALL SIN. How much SIN does Jesus' Blood destroy? ALL SIN… Nobody has a SIN PROBLEM in The Kingdom because ALL sin remains on earth. NO SIN transfers into The Kingdom, just like, NO SIN transfers into God's Heaven. As a new creation, sin is eliminated because of The Blood Sacrifice of Jesus Christ (2 Cor 5:17). Christ is the spotless Lamb of God who gave His life for the sins of the whole world. (John 3:16)

Scripture:
2 Cor 5:19-21 (NKJV)

[19] To wit, that God was in Christ, reconciling the world unto himself, not imputing their trespasses unto them (emphasis mine); and hath committed unto us the word of reconciliation.

17

[20] Now then we are ambassadors for Christ, as though God did beseech you by us: we pray you in Christ's stead, be ye reconciled to God.

[21] For he hath made him to be sin for us (emphasis mine), who knew no sin; that we might be made the righteousness of God in him.

THERE IS NO SIN IN THE KINGDOM OF JESUS CHRIST. Why is this? Because Jesus' Blood has destroyed ALL SIN in The Kingdom. Jesus is King of His Kingdom and His Blood has destroyed ALL SIN in His Kingdom. There is no condemnation because there is NO SIN. (Rom 8:1)

John, in the book of 1 John states in Chapter 1:9 the process by which Jesus keeps His body(the Church) pure.

1 John 1:9 (paraphrase mine)

John says, "if we confess our faults (sins, iniquities, trespasses), he (God) is faithful and will to be faithful and just to forgive us our faults (sins, iniquities, trespasses), and cleanse us from all unrighteousness ... (paraphrase mine)

1 John 1:9 Amplified Bible (AMP)

[9] If we [freely] admit that we have sinned and confess our sins, He is faithful and just [true to His own nature and promises], and will forgive our sins and cleanse us continually from all unrighteousness [our wrongdoing, everything not in conformity with His will and purpose].

We must remain pure by closing every open spiritual and human door in order to deny Satan a place to attack and destroy us. Some would still argue you still sinned. I say, what does it matter if that sin does not count? Psalms 32 says, Blessed is the man who's sins are forgiven. And Because of the Blood Covenant, ALL our sins are forgiven. (Rom 4:1-3, 5-8,13-17; Heb 10:14, Heb 10:16-18)

Add to that the statement of 2 Cor 5:21, "²¹ <u>For He (God) hath made Him (Christ) to be sin for us</u>, who knew no sin; that we might be made the righteousness of God in him…" (paraphrase mine)

Here we have the <u>Divine Exchange</u>. The Divine Exchange is what makes you SINLESS… Jesus takes your sins and gives you HIS RIGHTEOUSNESS.

If you are living a life of sin, you are not living Kingdom Life. Kingdom Life is about doing all the things that please Jesus, God our Father, and The Holy Spirit.

We are a Kingdom of transformed saints who have NO SIN against US.

The big stick is eliminated from the arsenal of judgment. You can never again be hit over the head with the sin issue. Hallelujah!!! Like Abraham, we have NO SIN placed against us (Rom 4:1-3). This all happened as a result of the Blood Covenant God established between himself and Abraham and now between Us and Jesus, and between Jesus and God The Father. We have a special bond and unity and because of Jesus' Blood we have Kingdom Life. NO SIN. You are SINLESS in The Kingdom of Jesus Christ.

We can take our minds off of the distractions in life that sin causes and place our complete focus on accomplishing what Jesus has called us to do. NO SIN. Original sin is NOT a FACTOR anymore. You can keep your sin if you want, but I am getting rid of mine. I call this <u>"The Divine Exchange"</u>, Jesus took my sin and gave me His righteousness.

The devil has implanted in our minds for too long that we are rejected by God. The truth is, that we are the BELOVED of the Father. We are not rejected due to SIN. There is NO SIN to reject. We are rejected because WE reject Jesus Christ as our savior (Jn 3:18) or we refuse to believe what God has spoken. We will deal with one scripture in Isaiah a little later that declares " God's ways are not our ways…". Getting the right perspective on sin is vital to our ability to establish Jesus' Kingdom on Earth as it is in heaven.

In the end, Jesus earthly Kingdom will be burned up with the rest of the world because Jesus' Kingdom will be transferred to God the Father. But now, as a part of Jesus' Earthly Kingdom, we have become the salt of the earth as stated:

Matthew 5:13

Ye are the salt of the earth: but if the salt have lost his savor, wherewith shall it be salted? it is thenceforth good for nothing, but to be cast out, and to be trodden under foot of men.

This saltiness is a result of being transferred into Jesus' Kingdom of Light.

John 8:12
Then spake Jesus again unto them, saying, I am the light of the world: he that followeth me shall not walk in darkness, but shall have the light of life.

John 9:5 As long as I am in the world, I am the light of the world.

Colosians 1:13 He has delivered us from the Kingdom of darkness and translated us into the Kingdom of his dear Son:

When Jesus ascended back to The Father after resurrection, Jesus' Kingdom became invisible to the natural eye, but immediately available to the children of Jesus' Kingdom, His disciples. We became Jesus' Kingdom on Earth while at the same time we became The Bride of Christ and The Church. As such, we provide a necessary element in the earth to offer Kingdom transformation to those who decide to accept Christ as Savior. We also become a powerful change agent for God to make the earth what He always wanted it to be, "heaven on earth." Since we are in the earth, we are the Salt of God to alter and influence the earth (Mt 5:13) daily. This change will make the earth compatible with the activities Jesus must have complete upon His return to earth to fulfill God's mandate of "thy kingdom come, thy will be done on earth as it is in heaven". At that time earth will become a representation of God's heavenly Kingdom. This is what the Hebrew nation was supposed to accomplish. Instead, they fell to the same contamination of Eve. Instead of eating from the tree of Life, she ate from the tree of Death and the world became dark.

Philippians 2:15 That ye may be blameless and harmless, the sons of God, without rebuke, in the midst of a crooked and perverse nation, among whom ye shine as lights in the world;

Matthew 5:13 Ye are the salt of the earth: but if the salt have lost his savor, wherewith shall it be salted? it is thenceforth good for nothing, but to be cast out, and to be trodden under foot of men.

We have a different taste and We have a different flavor for those who are ready to opt out of the devil's Kingdom

Revelation 16:10-11 And the fifth angel poured out his vial upon the seat of the beast; and his kingdom was full of darkness; and they gnawed their tongues for pain... 11) They blasphemed the God of heaven because of their pains and their sores, and did not repent of their deeds.

If these wanted to be delivered, they could have come into Jesus Kingdom

Colossians 1:13 Who hath delivered us from the power of darkness, and hath translated us into the kingdom of his dear Son:

Salt activates change to the fundamental flavor of earth life. The <u>Standards of Kingdom Life</u> make the divine difference in the responses of the people of God living and working "...on earth as it is in heaven...". Without this change, we are not truly representing Kingdom Life, we are simply earth citizens masquerading as someone representing Jesus as King.

<u>Psalm 110:1</u> The Lord said unto my Lord, Sit thou at my right hand, until I make thine enemies thy footstool.

KINGDOM LIFE DEMANDS THAT YOU GIVE UP EARTH LIFE

CHAPTER 3

KINGDOM LIFE IS NOT HUMAN LIFE

God's Greatest Potential for Humanity

Jesus made this statement about the Kingdom (Mark 4:10-12) [10] And when he was alone, they that were about him with the twelve asked of him the parable. [11] And he said unto them, <u>Unto you it is given to know the mystery of the kingdom of God</u>: but unto them that are without, all these things are done in parables: [12] That seeing they may see, and not perceive; and hearing they may hear, and not understand; lest at any time they should be converted, and their sins should be forgiven them.

As a Kingdom Citizen, my ultimate focus should be towards God's desire. You are a part of Jesus' Kingdom where eternal life has taken over your natural life. Our life focus now must center on becoming Just Like Jesus. This requires a drastic change in the way we live life and only makes sense in light of the transformation the Kingdom brings. As Rom 12:2 states, non-conformity to this world's ideology and methods based on Jesus' teachings brings us into conformity with Jesus' Kingdom. Kingdom Life is not started through physical works which means that the kingdoms of this world are not the same as The Kingdom of Jesus Christ (Mt 4:8-9). Human life is NOT the same as

Kingdom Life. (1 Cor 7:22-24) If you are living a life of sin, you are not living Kingdom Life. Those who have been bought with the price of Jesus' Blood Sacrifice serve Jesus, not the world. (Mt 4:8-9) The human (earthly) heart is not motivated like the heart of God. Jesus is not driven by the needs of the earth. Jesus is driven by the needs of His Father, our Creator. We should not be driven by needs outside our personal and Kingdom mandated realms either. In Jesus' world, Kingdom Life is the dominant force in everything (Jn 5:30). According to Isa 9:6-7, Jesus came as the Seed of David his father and fulfilled the prophetic word spoken by Isaiah the prophet to continue the Kingdom of Israel on earth and establish a worldwide Kingdom to replace the earths' structure. (Jn 7:41-42). Before Jesus' death, burial, and resurrection, the Kingdom of Israel could have no Gentiles included within it. (Mt 10:6; Mt 15:24; Jn 6:36-40). Jesus was sent only to the House of Israel. (Mt 15:23-24)

God gave Moses the Law as a sub-directive or bypass of the Blood Covenant of Abraham. Since Abraham's Covenant was the primary document for Jesus' arrival on earth. The Law was added as a parallel condition to the Blood Covenant until the Promised Seed should come because Israel broke the Covenant requirements within hours of Moses receiving them on Mt Siani (Gal 3:19). After Jesus' crucifixion, God ADDED the Abraham Blood Covenant to the Blood Covenant of Jesus for the Born Again believer. The result was God the Father Destroying the LAW forever which now makes a BETTER COVENANT for all. (Heb 7:22; 8:6; 12:24) Most Christians take these truths and place them in the same bag as any other part of the Bible thinking that those who follow the old testament and those that follow the new are on the same wavelength. Most people do not think the same way and minimize their authority in the earth when each covenant is treated the same.

The Law is NOT THE SAME as the Blood Covenant since it was developed 430 years after Abraham's original covenant with God. The Law is The Law of Moses, NOT The Blood Covenant of Abraham. Abraham's covenant is the preferred and controlling document in God's mind to bring into the earth. The Blood Covenant of Abraham remains the primary document and the enforcing directive for the Hebrew people, not The Law. Now that the purpose for The Law is complete, i.e....the sacrifice of Jesus on the Cross of Calvary, The Law has been discontinued in its entirety. All Kingdom behavior becomes subject to the Blood Covenant agreement of Jesus Christ. Jesus' Blood Covenant now eliminated any actions from The Law at all. Only the Blood Covenant Jesus established on the Cross of Calvary control the operation of the Kingdom. After Jesus' resurrection from the dead, Kingdom Life took leadership of all spiritual life under the authority of Jesus' Blood Covenant promise. Jesus Covenant now eliminates any argument the Pharisee or Sadducee spirit would have concerning the need for compliance with Moses directives like circumcision. The positions of the Pharisee and Sadducee were never authorized by The Law of Moses anyway. Only the office of the High Priest was ever given a position of authority and that was terminated and eliminated when Jesus became our High Priest (Heb 3:1). However, in keeping with the previously mentioned dual functions of scripture, because the Jewish people are God's special nation, (Rom 9) God still recognizes Israel as HIS own nation and people. They will not be lost.

Kingdom Life overrules earth life. Kingdom Life suspends the rules of physics, resistance and economics, etc. because Kingdom Life removes the barriers that limit productive and creative activity while establishing limitations on those things alone that violate God's supernatural structure. Whatever is good and kind and holy, worthy of honor, lovely, just, etc... become the guiding light. (Col 3:5-14) The Law only works to evaluate the flesh life here on earth, it does not work with Kingdom Life.

Since we live in a dual reality, in the Kingdom there is no hate or sin and Jesus' blood sacrifice destroyed ALL SIN FOREVER in The Kingdom. Therefore SIN does NOT exist. On earth sin still exists because Satan is the god of this world. So, you must make a choice. Are you a citizen of The Kingdom or are you a citizen of the earth. In the Kingdom there is no inequality; in the Kingdom everything that God has is available to you and inside you (Jn 14:17-23; Jn 17:14-29). In the Kingdom there is no black nor white, no color nor nationality, there is no young or old, there is no rich, nor poor in the Kingdom. In the Kingdom everyone is a son of God because there are no sexes in The Kingdom. Everything Jesus can do, YOU can do also. ALL the ABILITIES of GOD are yours. In The Kingdom the Church does not exist, we go back to temple or synagogue worship. We have member saints who are Sons of God because Jesus is the ONLY King and leader. In The Kingdom everyone is anointed all the time. In The Kingdom there are unlimited positions for activity and production. In The Kingdom there is only ONE leader. In The Kingdom ALL gifts, talents, and abilities are ACTIVE ALL the time in EVERYBODY. Like Jesus said, "you are in the world, but not OF the world…" Kingdom Life is all about becoming just like Jesus. Everything else is secondary to your transformation into a complete son of God. Galatians says it this way;

Galatians 3:23-29, Ch 4:1-7 (NKJV)

[23] But before faith came, we were kept under the law, shut up unto the faith which should afterwards be revealed. [24] Wherefore the <u>law was our schoolmaster</u> to bring us unto Christ, that we might be justified by faith. [25] But after that faith is come, <u>we are no longer under a schoolmaster</u>. [26] For ye are all the children of God by faith in Christ Jesus. [27] For as many of you as have been baptized into Christ have put on Christ.

[28] There is neither Jew nor Greek, there is neither bond nor free, there is neither male nor female: for ye are all one in Christ Jesus. [29] And if ye be Christ's, then are ye Abraham's seed, and heirs according to the promise.

Gal 4:1-7

4 Now I say, That the heir, as long as he is a child, differs nothing from a servant, though he be lord of all; [2] But is under tutors and governors until the time appointed of the father. [3] Even so we, when we were children, were in bondage under the elements of the world: [4] But when the fullness of the time was come, God sent forth his Son, made of a

woman, made under the law,[5] To redeem them that were under the law, that we might receive the <u>adoption of sons</u>.[6] And <u>because ye are sons</u>, God hath sent forth the Spirit of his Son into your hearts, crying, Abba, Father.[7] Wherefore thou art <u>no more a servant, but a son</u>; and if a son, <u>then an heir of God through Christ</u> Jesus.

John 17:14-16 all believers "are not of this world even as I am not of this world".

Thus we as Christians are no longer <u>Human</u> by definition. Instead we have been declared DIVINE just like Jesus as Sons of God, family! Rev 5:10 tells us that God said, "…And hast made us unto our God kings and priests: and we shall reign on the earth."

All spiritual transactions are processed through The Kingdom from the Spirit of God inside of you. You must be "Born Again to experience the things of The Kingdom" (Jn 3:3) and not ALL spiritual actions are of God.

There is NOTHING DEAD in Jesus' Kingdom. The word says that Jesus came to bring life! (Jn 10:10) Everything from God has LIFE.

Kingdom Life is a life spent chasing God all the time. Kingdom Life is a life spent doing all that can be done to demonstrate Jesus on Earth while you become just like him.

The Human Community does not represent The Kingdom no matter how well ordered it may seem. Underneath the surface of humanity is that old sin nature called original sin. This nature separates humanity from God our Creator. Only those who have been washed in the Blood of Jesus Christ thus accepting His covenant can have Kingdom Life. Kingdom Life is a life of VALUE. You are the Beloved of the Lord. Animals, fish, even the earth do not take priority over our relationship with God the Creator. According to the book of Genesis, everything made was to be used for the existence of mankind. Nothing on earth is more valuable than mankind (Gen 9:1-3). What a stark contrast to the mindset of today's social structure. The worlds' cry is to save everything but the human element. That mindset has led the world into destruction through drugs, alcohol, human trafficking, war, starvation, and hate as man determines the value of a soul rather than using God's standards. Kingdom Life requires that earth life be transformed into God Life (Zoe) in order for The Kingdom to operate. (John 3:3)

During the Transformation phase of Kingdom Life there will be moments of weakness when we desire to return to the human life we have given up. Like the Hebrew children leaving Egypt we may desire to return to the human element for something familiar. Transformation can be a challenging process; However, we MUST overcome this challenge. Remember in Revelations 2 the reward is only given to, "he who overcomes." (Rev 2:7, 17,26)

Relationship with God the Father through Jesus establishes Kingdom Life. Only those who are pursuing a deeper, more real and complete relationship with God our Creator are ready to establish Kingdom Life fully. All areas of our human existence must be transformed to completely embrace Kingdom Life. For those who say this cannot be done we must remember Jesus on the Mount of Transfiguration. (Mt 17:1-8) Jesus not only achieved Kingdom Life status, but He also achieved resurrection status by being transfigured with a resurrection body even before he died on the Cross. Jesus also received his white robe and had God the Father declare HIS Son pleasing. Jesus interacted with the ALIVE saints Moses and Elijah while still standing on earth... Jesus demonstrated Kingdom Life while on earth in a HUMAN BODY. Jesus said we will do greater things than he has done (Jn 14:12).

In order to do more than Jesus, we must understand that God the Father Lives IN US all the time. (Jn 14:15-26) 1 Cor 2:16 says, " we have the mind of Christ".

Transfiguration and Transformation according to Strong's dictionary… are the same word. Strong's ref. 3339 states the definition, "…as a completely changed form and appearance into a more beautiful or spiritual state; a change in form or appearance, metamorphosis; an exalting, glorifying, or spiritual change."

In Kingdom Life, transformation primarily takes place inside the SOUL. The body is a robot for the most part, we have trained it to respond as we desire because of the many habits and desires we have embraced during our human existence. Our Spirit man is transformed because of Salvation, "…the old man has gone, behold the new man has come…" (Col 3:9, Eph 4:22, 2 Cor 5:17) Paul also identified the functions of our human existence as Spirit, Soul and Body (1 Thes 5:23). These areas of our developmental man are the primary targets of the devil's influence to stop or hinder or slow down our full Transformation into the "… fullness of the measure and stature of Christ…" (Eph 4:13b) 99% of our effort will be to overcome and develop the Soul to accept the "the fullness of the stature and measure of Christ Jesus". We trained our soul man to like the way we live, the way we think, our personal dreams and desire, and to pursue life's opportunities in order to get what we want. We trained the soul to like earth life! Whether we did it quickly or slowly does not matter. Now those same cravings, appetites, desires and habits are fighting to control whether we achieve the Godly status destined for us before we eliminate our humanity. No wonder this is such a struggle. Our soul becomes our enemy to challenge and destroy our hopes of becoming just like Jesus because the devil gives support and reinforcements to the old man from ALL levels.

Our soul is comprised of our will, emotions, and intellect or mind. These three areas gang up on us to defeat the transformative changes that will cause us to become fully Jesus in every level of life.

How you think matters, how you believe matters, what you choose to do matters, and what you choose to agree with matters in every level of life. The same goes for what you choose NOT to agree with. Nothing is too small on this table.

Everything that does not line up with Biblical principles and behavior must be rejected completely to receive total authority we must follow these scriptural examples which say, "I only speak that which I have heard my Father say and only do which I see my Father do…" (Jn 5, Jn 8:34-38, Jn 14:7).

CHAPTER 4

TRANSFORMATION

Thy Kingdom Come, Thy Will be Done

DUAL CITIZENSHIP

It is not possible to have an earthly mindset and do what God desires to be done to transform the earth. Everything the Bible talks about requires a full and complete transformation of our human soul/mindset allowing metamorphosis. For us to become just like Jesus, this is the only way. This is the only way we will do "the greater things" Jesus spoke about. (Jn 14:10-12)

THE NEW TESTAMENT ONLY MAKES SENSE IN LIGHT OF METAMORPHOSIS

Adam was not offered transformation in his lifetime. Adam was not infused with the LIFE of JESUS since God the Father was already with him daily. If he had been offered Christ, Adam would not have sinned and given the earth to Satan. With this understanding we must enter into a NEW way of thinking about our salvation. We must begin to see our salvation from a heavenly point of view instead of an earthly point of view.

Unlike James & John who wanted Jesus to give them authority to call down fire from heaven (Lk 9:51-56), death is not a kingdom activity. Unlike Judas who tried to force Jesus into his way of handling things before going to the Cross, manipulation is not a Kingdom activity.

Instead we see Jesus operating in agreement with The Father all the time. John, James, and Judas were operating from an earthly mindset. (Jn.18:1-6)

It is no longer as important to know what is changing on earth as it is to know what is changing in heaven. Though we are limited by our physical body, the body of Christ is becoming just like Jesus every day. We must accept this charge and partnership for transformation to process 100%. Do <u>Not Demand</u> that God make you a BETTER HUMAN. Instead, demand that we become much more aggressive in our pursuit of becoming the likeness of Christ. What does that look like?

<u>Firstly</u>, my prayer life must be the number one priority during my day. Seeking after ALL of God is vital, but hearing God is most important (Jn 10:1-5). My sheep hear my voice… I must shift from emphasizing a sin life to living a Godly life.

<u>Secondly</u>, we must value scripture above our way of thinking. The transformation process has already been activated, now we must allow that process to take over every area of our being.

Nicodemus spoke to Jesus in a way that responded to earth life. Jesus, assuming that Nicodemus was a spiritual person, since he was a priest, responded to him like he understood Kingdom Life. Therefore, Jesus went on to talk about Kingdom Life (Jn 18:24-37; 3:1-12) and Nicodemus was not able to understand what Jesus meant by what he said. The same thing is happening to us. We are talking to God about earth life, when God is talking to us about Kingdom Life and we cannot understand what he means by what he says and we become confused. Every word Jesus spoke in the New Testament is about <u>Kingdom Life</u>; therefore we must shift our thinking and lifestyle to a heavenly position in order to understand what God is saying about the earth.

God is not changing heaven....God is changing earth

God's ways are not our ways on earth yet, but for the believer, GOD'S ways <u>Must Become</u> OUR Ways. In heaven you don't speak, you just think, while on earth our words declare God's desires for our lives. Isa 55:8-9

Kingdom mindsets require having the same motives and methods Jesus demonstrated to Pilate. This requires a melt-down, a diminishing, a removing of <u>how we think</u>, Jesus way of thinking must become greater while our way becomes less dominant literally. Metamorphosis is the meltdown, a meltdown of who, why, and what you used to be. The Pressures of life will make this happen literally. We will be left thinking how did God do that in me. Unexpectedly God will transition you into another realm of activity and you will not even know you have changed.

What was the purpose of Jesus being taken to Pilate? The Bible declares that if Satan had known, he would not have crucified the Lord of Glory. (1 Cor 2:8-11) Satan did not know he was sealing his doom by crucifying Jesus. God did! This was <u>KINGDOM THINKING.</u> We are authorized to know everything God knows – Mk 4:11, 1 Cor 2:16, Rev 10:7. The mysteries are available to us. We are not just smart people. God is already revealing to HIS people what he knows, if we will actively accept his process as our goal in life, God will give us insight.

Jesus said it... Jn 18: 37 - "...to this end was I born..."

Jesus knew why he was on earth. You were not <u>born-again</u> to stay human. You were born again to become the exact image and likeness of Jesus Christ our savior – Rom 8:29

Kingdom Life is what we are going to be living when Jesus sets up His Kingdom on earth

On the Mount of Transfiguration, Jesus showed us what our end will be. Most people think this can only happen in heaven, I say Jesus demonstrated what can happen on earth, and therefore the proof of supernatural life begins now.

Matthew 17 (KJV)

1 And after six days Jesus taketh Peter, James, and John his brother, and bringeth them up into an high mountain apart,

2 And was transfigured before them: and his face did shine as the sun, and his raiment was white as the light.

3 And, behold, there appeared unto them Moses and Elias [Elijah] talking with him.

4 Then answered Peter, and said unto Jesus, Lord, it is good for us to be here: if thou wilt, let us make here three tabernacles; one for thee, and one for Moses, and one for Elias [Elijah].

5 While he yet spake, behold, a bright cloud overshadowed them: and behold a voice out of the cloud, which said, This is my beloved Son, in whom I am well pleased; hear ye him.

Jesus was on earth during this event. He had no supernatural activity coming out of His voice or hands, yet Jesus is able to contact God the

Father as he prays for direction for the events of the coming days. Before the prayer is over Jesus is transfigured before them and his face begins to shine as the sun, and his raiment was white as the light. Then Moses and Elijah appear first with information about what is going to happen. Mind you, all this is happening during a PRAYER SESSION. Jesus is asking for direction from His Father for his mission. Then God the Father shows up and joins the conversation while hiding in a cloud and confirms what Moses and Elijah have already told Jesus.

What happens during YOUR prayer time? Additionally, during the whole conversation Jesus is changed into his <u>Glorified Body</u> <u>before He was crucified!</u>

What do you think of that? Wow... This sheds light on what God has done to transition our Human life into Kingdom Life. Wow... We are not left to face life's issues without authority to bring change. Mark 4:11 tells us that "... Unto you it is given to know the mystery of the kingdom of God: but unto them that are without, all these things are done in parables."

Kingdom Life is the life believers have when they have accepted the death, burial, and resurrection of Jesus Christ as Lord and savior!

"Kingdom Life is easy to enter, but it is not easy to fully embrace and understand"

Most ministries teach a gospel that insists that we remain HUMAN and never achieve an intimate relationship with The Father until we reach heaven. If a person attempts to increase his or her Godly position, most ministries will shut them down or place them in a position of being weird. As such, most churches fail to identify the qualities that make our spiritual life dynamic. We are expected not to walk past the human boundary. Supernatural demonstrations are not accepted as a sign of good Christianity. Modeling life in the manner Jesus demonstrated is suspect. Therefore believers do not grow in the manner Kingdom Life requires.

In a sense, we become like Jerusalem in Jesus day, "…Jerusalem, Jerusalem, if you had known the one who was coming…"(Mt 23:37)

Kingdom Life versus human life is a complex mixture. What you were is not who you are any more and what you are becoming is not fully completed in a definable mental package. (1 Cor 13:12) How you pursue your relationship with Jesus makes a huge difference in this process.

> "Many things about the Kingdom are caught by example while being taught by The Holy Spirit."

When you become born again, you accept a family number behind Jesus. Rom 8:29 says, "…that he might be the first born of many brotherin…" In this process you become the 2nd, 3rd, 4th, or 5th born behind Jesus. The difference is, ONLY Jesus' Blood can forgive sin. Jesus is the first born among many brethren so that makes you a son just like Jesus before God our Father.

Romans 8:29 - For whom he did foreknow, he also did predestinate to be conformed to the image of his Son, that he might be the firstborn among many brethren.

Jesus made the Divine Exchange when we entered Kingdom Life

2 Corinthians 5:17-21

[17] Therefore if any man be in Christ, he is a new creature: old things are passed away; behold, all things are become new. [18] And all things are of God, who hath reconciled us to himself by Jesus Christ, and hath given to us the ministry of reconciliation; [19] To wit, that God was in Christ, reconciling the world unto himself, not imputing their trespasses unto

them; and hath committed unto us the word of reconciliation.[20] Now then we are ambassadors for Christ, as though God did beseech you by us: we pray you in Christ's stead, be ye reconciled to God. [21] For he hath made him to be sin for us, who knew no sin; that we might be made the righteousness of God in him.

As soon as you entered salvation you became a new creation… Transformation and Metamorphosis began within your DNA. You were happy, your daily load in life was light and you felt on top of the world even though the world was the same. You experienced a new dimension of life. You did not understand it but you were glad to have it. Some of us stay in that realm for days, others for months or years. Eventually that feeling of euphoria dwindles and we, as some say, "come down to earth". THAT is Kingdom Life declaring "I'M HERE". God the Father converts your DNA into HIS DNA and stamps you by the Holy Spirit as HIS son and a member of the Kingdom. (Eph 1:13) Jesus takes away ALL SIN, INIQUITY, and TRESPASSES from your life and makes you a new member of God the Father's family and a son of God. (Jn 1:12) Romans 8:1-5 declares you free from shame and guilt as you start to understand that God is not mad at you anymore. All things have become new! The Blood of Jesus has done it's job! This transaction activates the transformation process as Jesus takes your sins and gives you HIS righteousness forever. You become a sinless son of Jehovah God as stated in 1 Jn 3:1. This is the DIVINE EXCHANGE. You are no longer a sinner saved by grace. Now you are a SINLESS son of Jehovah God. Hallelujah!

Immediately you have "the mind of Christ" available to you (1 Cor 2:16) and you have authorization to know "the mysteries of the Kingdom". (Mk 4:11) Any other way of thinking causes us to go astray in a human manner. Sometimes we don't ask for the mysteries of the Kingdom, we start asking for STUFF. Like make me rich, heal me, save my brother, sister, son, etc. But where is our hunger for Kingdom Life.

Instead of asking for the Wisdom of Jesus or desiring to know how God operates His Kingdom, we are left alone to figure this out for ourselves. Instead of being disconnected from the earth, we are reconnected by returning to our most familiar desires. We act this way because we are taught this way.

Ignorantly we repeat human/earthly actions instead of Godly/Kingdom Actions. Ignorantly we stay connected to the earth where only 2 things happen. You are born and then you die. That's it for earth life. There are no supernatural markings to earth life. Having a photo-graphic memory is nothing in the Kingdom. On earth, you still have to read before you can remember. In the Kingdom you know before it is written. Praise God! God CREATES, he does not replicate. We are satisfied following what others have already done instead of doing what has never been thought of before. Kingdom Life is NOT human life. Yet, there is a process to be followed.

According to Pat Robertson, "Somehow we fail to take seriously the fact that the Kingdom of God is the central teaching of Jesus...Indeed He described such teaching as His ultimate purpose: "I must preach about God's kingdom to other towns too… this is why I was sent."(The Secret Kingdom, pg 16)

<u>Kingdom Life must change human life</u>. To be usable by our King, Jesus Christ, our lives are no longer our own. The Kingdom focuses on this specific activity for two reasons. (1) To establish ownership of you as its personal citizen and (2) to overthrow the influence of Satan within The Kingdom itself. This second action declares there are no spies in the Kingdom. <u>As we begin to act like Jesus we return ownership of the earth to God</u>. Because we are willing to give our portion into God's authority, Jesus establishes His Kingdom on earth right now.

All disputes over our earth are settled by God because of your New Birth
(Jude 8-13)

KINGDOM LIFE IS NOW

We start and complete the transition into Kingdom Life while we are on earth. The return of Christ depends on a certain remnant becoming "the fullness of the measure and stature of Christ" TODAY. A certain number of "Kingdom Nations" must be established before Jesus will be released from heaven (Acts3:19-21). Most Christians call this the second coming or RETURN of Christ. We have shifted from the "Church Age" to the "Kingdom Establishing Age." (Bishop Bill Hamon – Apostles', Prophets and Coming Moves of God) To accomplish this we, as the body of Christ, must develop a Kingdom Mentality greater than our earthly mentality. It takes all of God to fix all of mankind. God has always known what it takes to position mankind in the right location.

Gen 2:18 says, "…and the Lord God said, it is not good that the man should be alone; I will make him an help meet for him…" God knew that Adam could not be satisfied as a man without Eve. God also knows that for man to be at rest, man must have Kingdom Life. Kingdom Life will allow the born again man to think like Jesus, act like Jesus, talk like Jesus, and walk like Jesus every day. Man can not accomplish this by his desires (Mt 4:2-4) and think that he is accomplishing God's purpose in the earth.

Jesus lived in 2 worlds not 1. We live in 2 worlds, not 1. (Jn 17:14-16) We are the catalyst that will bring Jesus back to earth and establish His full earthly residence and divine rule. The destruction of sinfulness in the world will not bring Jesus back.

Jesus is not coming back because the world is sooooo bad. The second coming is not based on a Sodom and Gomorrah story. The second coming is based on a people, called by <u>Jesus' name</u> that looks like, walks like, talks like, thinks like, and acts like Jesus. Well what about The Book of Revelations? Yes there are some bad things going to happen, but that is not what brings Jesus back to earth. Jesus' bride, prepared for the wedding day is what brings Jesus back to earth INVISIBLY first... We MUST be prepared for the wedding. To such an end, we must be ready for marriage at any moment. That means we cannot be broken, despondent, discouraged, or unmotivated at his return! Life will be GOOD and full of joy, peace and power (Rom 15:13). This is the time Jesus brings his Bride home invisibly. for Jesus to establish His Kingdom on earth. This is only the time He takes His bride home.

Kingdom Life is preparation for The Wedding of the Bride.

A certain mindset must be established before that day can come. You get all the goodies after the wedding night has been completed. Before that day you just look good, smell good, smile a lot, receive compliments, eat cake, and drink a toast to the celebration of a long awaited union with your master.

The "Mindset of Kingdom Life" requires an orderly transition for us to be transformed into the <u>perfect mate for Christ</u>. This is not just living right and being Holy. We must fundamentally begin to resemble the likeness of Christ. Then, in our Jesus state, we are ready, like a Bride, for total and complete union with Christ on earth before we go to heaven. Ruling with Christ, using HIS authority, is a factor of becoming the exact image of Christ on earth. (Col 2:9-11) Our Bibles are instructions on how to become complete in Christ before going to heaven. Our goal, our job, our purpose is to become the fullness of the measure and stature of Christ right now. We are not waiting to get to heaven, we are going to the "Mount of Transfiguration" for that experience right now. Are you ready?

HUMAN VALUE

On earth human value is mostly determined by what you can produce or how you can contribute to the accomplishment of the goals established or the successful completion of outcomes and situations. In Kingdom Life this is not true. Kingdom Life gives every person the same number of abilities, skills, understanding, revelation, wisdom, etc. Why? Every believer is a son of God. God does not assign responsibility because of talent, intelligence, or possessions. God assigns responsibility because His need is for us is to be completely obedient. As a result, God gives us credit for accomplishment. Attempting to prove my worth without the core value of obedience renders us unusable.

The greatest perpetrators of judgment between humans on earth are the acts of competition. I compare what you did to what I did and according to earth values that makes you better than me. In Kingdom Life that is not how value is determined. If you are taller, stronger, more intelligent, funnier, a better smile, more appealing physically, makes no difference to Jesus or the Father when it comes to selection or need. The issue is our obedience. Remember the parable in Mt 21:28-32 Jesus talks about two sons. The Father went to one son and said, " Go into the fields and the son said I will not. Then the Father went to the other son and said, Go into the fields and the son said, I will. But he did not go. Instead, the son who said he would not go went, and the son who said I will go did not. Jesus then said, Who did the will of his Father?" The son who went did do the will of his Father because he was OBEDIENT.

Other statements of scripture that apply this truth are found in Galatians 3:28, and Colossians 3:11. The value of Kingdom Life is your obedience to the plan of God, not your skill, intelligence, physical attribute, or wealth. God is looking for those who will submit and who will obey His directives on a 24 hour basis. The closer we come to this bench mark, the more we receive from heaven's store to accomplish what The Kingdom needs to have happen.

The human perspective on qualification is irrelevant to positioning and ability to accomplish the job the Kingdom needs done. This is why God takes the foolish things to confound the wise in establishing the message and work of the Kingdom in every aspect. God will allow failure if that shows his divine provision and protection in your life, but God will not make you a failure nor weak to put you in that position. Our humanity will make the selection for us. We struggle and sweat to gain recognition in this life or to attain possessions to prove we are worth acceptance only to lose those assets and fall out of the race to be somebody in the eyes of humanity. Instead, God looks at you as having become a primary candidate for the infusion of His presence and power when you struggle in this way. Failing isn't the objective, but your attitude and humility is the winning key to gaining God's attention in your life. The indispensable stages of respect are established in this manner.

Kingdom Life is not measured by Human standards. As the church or as God's people we must begin to make God's Ways our ways right now in order to achieve our greatest relationship with God.

WE MUST START ASKING FOR TRANSFORMATION TODAY.
GOD DOES NOT TREAT YOU LIKE MAN TREATS YOU

CHAPTER 5

KINGDOM LIFE IS NOT CHURCH LIFE

God's Mandate for the Ekklesia Before
Leaving Earth

The Church is the Body and the Kingdom is the territory of Jesus. From the beginning, God's design for ruling and reigning in the earth was centered on his Kingdom concepts. Adam and Eve were to subdue the earth and repopulate the existing lands so that a God race would rule over everything that God had created. After the need for Jesus to redeem the people of God's Kingdom was obvious, God sent himself as the Holy Spirit to oversee the individual people who would eventually replace Jesus on earth and called them the Ekklesia or called out ones. Jesus then set these Ekklesia members into a unit or group to be trained by a five member leadership panel under the direction of The Holy Spirit. The sole purpose was to Transform each member of this group now called the Church into "...the fullness of the measure and stature of Christ..." (Eph 4:13); We must become members that have been fully transformed into Jesus image and function as Jesus in the earth on a daily basis. This fundamental change starts at SALVATION. The Kingdom is a billion times larger than the "World Wide Church." This being the case, Kingdom Life includes ALL legitimate Ekklesia members established by God on planet earth.

The Kingdom is not many entities coming together as one, but one entity divided into many groups and members for the purpose of transforming the world into the full image of Jesus Christ.

That makes <u>church life a sub-culture</u> to <u>Kingdom Life</u> in the same way that <u>The Law of Moses is a sub-directive to The Abrahamic Covenant.</u> The Law NEVER took precedence over The Abrahamic Covenant and does not take precedence over The Kingdom of Jesus Christ. The main difference is that there is one leader over the Kingdom instead of many leaders/trainers in the church. Jesus is the King and He has set the fivefold leadership team as His designated trainers in the church. Jesus then, remains King over His entire body (Eph 4:11-13). Jesus is the ONLY VICAR to the church. Everyone in the church has the same abilities with differing positions for management purposes. Yet, we as the Church seem to become the physical property of the human leader instead of the property of Jesus Christ. As leaders, we cannot allow any member to think that we are the final answer. We MUST insist that the Ekklesia always know they MUST FIND THE FINAL ANSWER IN JESUS through the HOLY SCRIPTURE. As Paul the Apostle says, "…Is Christ divided?…" (1 Cor 1:13). And although each church is supposed to reflect Jesus in HIS completeness, we "who are being transformed" must declare our transformation in process over and over again. My humanity is being swallowed up as I become the exact image of Jesus (Rom 8:29). This ideology must be my purpose every day.

Kingdom Life, therefore, is not church life because the church has thrown out the expectation of becoming the divine replication of Christ as a daily goal.

The Church of Jesus Christ was birthed by supernatural activity, but now the church of the earth denies the same supernatural activity that birthed her. Then we declare this supernatural activity demonic or heretical at its core. If you act like Jesus you will be persecuted like Jesus, but does our love and grace ethic cause us to be better humans or more like Jesus. The Church limits what a Christian can do as a representative of Christ's Kingdom instead of expanding what we do as a representation of the Kingdom.

In Matthew 20:21 we find the mother of the Apostles James and John, sons of Zebedee coming to Jesus with a request. "Make my two sons to sit, one on the right and one on the left in your Kingdom."(Paraphrase mine) Jesus had been teaching on The Kingdom and this mother had understood that an opportunity was going to be available for advancement. She wanted a place for her boys to get in on the deal. Jesus taught about His Kingdom differently than he taught about His Father's Kingdom. These are two different places. This mother understood the separation. Jesus does not demand a church to have miracles, signs, and wonders daily, but no hunger for a miracle, sign or wonder at all is a sign that the light has gone out. <u>Greater things than Jesus has done</u> must be our motivation and daily mantra. (Jn 14:12)

The Church cannot produce what Jesus has said without HIM... Yet we insist on doing the King's work all by ourselves. "Without a vision the people wonder aimlessly around. We come up with a slogan and put it on the wall, but where is the proof of the slogan? The Bible goes on to say that we must seek that vision from God through a Prophetic encounter in order to have clarity (Ezek 7:26). But the earthly church continues doing business WITHOUT REQUIRING OF ITSELF visible signs of the Life of Christ its King. The ultimate vanity and pride is to reject becoming like Jesus. My hunger is demonstrated when I actively go out the doors of the church and lay hands on the sick expecting healing and I lay hands on people to receive what they need before they see it or say it. By doing this, I put my life and reputation on the line for Christ to verify the fact that I am being transformed.

We have many signs of earth life and human life, but no signs of Kingdom Life as Jesus requires. Jesus doesn't require a miracle every day, but He does require some supernatural activity of His <u>life-giving</u> presence in his people, the Ekklesia and in His ministers.

Where are the training opportunities for Christians to learn how to become "the fullness of the measure and stature of Christ". Our Bible colleges and theological centers produce no vision, no Demonstration and no Learning process to become just like Jesus. Man does not know what is NOT good for him, only God does. To this point Christians (the ekklesia) and the church perish. I have separated the individual Christian from a single organized church body because this is how we operate. We don't see the two as the same unit when in fact they are the same.

John 10:16 says, "And other sheep I have, which are not of this fold: them also I must bring, and they shall hear my voice; and there shall be one fold, and one shepherd." Is this future or current?

These believers belong to Jesus' Kingdom also, even though they are not a part of the organized Church of the west. Yet with the current paradigm of the American Christian church these groups are ignored or considered the infamous "others" who are not of us. I believe we now call them "the persecuted church" or we make them a mission's project. In America an organization called American Center for Law and Justice or ACLJ has brought attention to these other Christian communities in the world unknown to Americans and have offered them legal representation. These saints have received Jesus as savior and are a part of Jesus' Kingdom just like you and I, but the concept of church is far from them because they are the Ekklesia representing Jesus Kingdom though not designated a Church. These do not nor do they want to function in a manner like the American church structure demands. Yet they are Kingdom citizens just like you and me. Jesus' Kingdom is bigger than the Church.

Because the church has mostly chosen to align itself with the earth and the world as a humanitarian group, most of the organized church groups give no significant position to other groups Jesus calls "His Body" and as such serve to divide Christ' body. Now we can see how Kingdom principles unify believers rather than that of individual church groups. This one commission declares as the Lord's Prayer,"... thy kingdom come thy will be done..." Mt 6:9-15 and Rev 11:15, "...the kingdoms of this world have and are become the Kingdoms of our Lord and His Christ"

Church life as we know it is too limited, too segmented, too dysfunctional to be The Kingdom. The Kingdom began under the direction and authority of The Holy Spirit. Jesus said "I must go away before He (The Holy Spirit) would come"(John 16:7-15). Then Jesus said, "...I send the promise of my Father upon you..." (Lk 24:49). Before the Apostles died, they told the leaders that wolves would come into the church to destroy its purity and purpose. And that is exactly what happened in those early days. This will again if we are not fully committed to being transformed into Kingdom Life.

Judaizes were leaders who disregarded the teachings of the disciples about the immerging Church and Kingdom of Christ. These wanted to keep the Solomaic Temple Worship and the laws as the symbol of salvation instead of the Cross of Jesus Christ. Because of this, wolves (Judaizes) contaminated the message being preached to the world about Christ Jesus. (2 Pt 3:2-5)

When the Canon, which established our Biblical Text, was ready to be solidified, there were 318 Bishops (called Popes by translation) in attendance of the Counsel of Nicea. Constantine, a relatively new

Christian and Emperor of the Roman Empire, was the director of this counsel and was used by God to establish the Divine position of Christ as savior and Lord. As such, God blessed Constantine to save the remainder of Christians from extinction at the hands of the Diocletian the previous Emperor of Rome. Is history repeating itself through terrorism? Is the church under threat? Constantine oversaw the Council in 325 A.D. and established the 66 books of the Bible (Yale Internet Courses-#1-8 Constantine and The Early Church) after several other issues were satisfactorily concluded concerning the Divinity of Christ. In 440 A.D. Pope Leo asserts his power over all the other Bishops stating he had the "Power of the Keys". With this statement being unopposed by the other Bishops, Leo I took control of the church in Rome and began the direction which made the church catholic and returned the church back to the Pharisee/Sadducee/Sanhedrin methods of Jesus day. Later, Martin Luther would establish the Protestant churches after receiving the revelation that the "just shall live by faith," an action which moved the church needle in the right direction for Kingdom Life. Overall, the Church leaders understood that the earth is Jesus' Kingdom and were moving to make it a completed fact. Unfortunately, this move was not not lead by the Spirit of God to require the mandatory submission of the people to the Roman Pope as voted in 1073 A.D. These things Jesus would have never done. If this were Jesus intention, he would have done so before leaving earth the first time. Instead, Jesus would have overridden the Sanhedrin and Pharisee/Sadducee regimes of His day to establish the plans of God for the future. Certainly after his resurrection Jesus would have just wiped out all opposition to God's plans. However, Jesus did not do this because that was not the way God the Father intended people's choices to be made. Were too small a group to control the numbers of unchanged people in the land. (Ex 23:29-33) Consequently, all who accepted Jesus should have been voluntary participants in order for truth and true change to become foremost in the land. Maybe in hindsight we can see this is true.

Acts 15:1-9 says this, let's read:

Acts 15 ...consolidate all verses to 11

1 And certain men which came down from Judaea taught the brethren, and said, Except ye be circumcised after the manner of Moses, ye cannot be saved.

² When therefore Paul and Barnabas had no small dissension and disputation with them, they determined that Paul and Barnabas, and certain other of them, should go up to Jerusalem unto the apostles and elders about this question.

³ And being brought on their way by the church, they passed through Phenice and Samaria, declaring the conversion of the Gentiles: and they caused great joy unto all the brethren.

⁴ And when they were come to Jerusalem, they were received of the church, and of the apostles and elders, and they declared all things that God had done with them.

⁵ But there rose up certain of the sect of the Pharisees which believed, saying, That it was needful to circumcise them, and to command them to keep the law of Moses.

⁶ And the apostles and elders came together for to consider this matter.

⁷ And when there had been much disputing, Peter rose up, and said unto them, Men and brethren, ye know how that a good while ago God made choice among us, that the Gentiles by my mouth should hear the word of the gospel, and believe.

⁸ And God, which knoweth the hearts, bare them witness, giving them the Holy Ghost, even as he did unto us;

⁹ And put no difference between us and them, purifying their hearts by faith.

[10] Now therefore why tempt ye God, to put a yoke upon the neck of the disciples, which neither our fathers nor we were able to bear?

[11] But we believe that through the grace of the LORD Jesus Christ we shall be saved, even as they.

Just as the Pharisee and Sadducee voices were a strong challenge to Jesus in an attempt to stop him from completing the will of God, these same types of voices continued to break apart the New Testament Church and became a contaminate to the organization. Power and pride destroyed the pure flow of truth. This process took over a 1000 years to become dominant, but eventually it dragged the gospel message back to the OLD ideology of the past which caused Israel to lose its relationship with God in the first place. Now the same thinking is causing the New Testament church to divide. Let's read further.

[15] And to this agree the words of the prophets; as it is written,

[16] After this I will return, and will build again the tabernacle of David, which is fallen down; and I will build again the ruins thereof, and I will set it up:

[17] That the residue of men might seek after the Lord, and all the Gentiles, upon whom my name is called, saith the Lord, who doeth all these things.

[18] Known unto God are all his works from the beginning of the world.

[19] Wherefore my sentence is, that we trouble not them, which from among the Gentiles are turned to God:

[20] But that we write unto them, that they abstain from pollutions of idols, and from fornication, and from things strangled, and from blood.

As we just read, we can see that the reintroduction of circumcision would cause divisive argumentation in the Book of Acts and a separation of the Gentile church from the Newly Born Again Church. These old ideologies allowed actions and laws to be implemented that Jesus never intended. These were tag-a-longs in the freshly renewed Spirit of the gentile believers. These issues caused rejection of the freedoms Christ's Blood had given them. Without these new truths, the gentiles believer would not accept the full measure that Christ's redemption gave them. (Acts 15:4-5, 6-12, 19-25) We see this same pattern continued by using divisive ideology with God's people around the world.

It was here that the Seeds of Division began because there was no cleansing of "the leaven of the Pharisees' "(Mt 16:12) as they carried the contaminating voice and doctrine of past processes into the New Testament Church Life. Unfortunately, these voices have remained a major problem to distort and disrupt the purity of The Gospel message among gentile believers even today.

Kingdom Life brings UNITY not division into the Church because there is ONE HEAD.

²² Then pleased it the apostles and elders with the whole church, to send chosen men of their own company to Antioch with Paul and Barnabas; namely, Judas surnamed Barnabas and Silas, chief men among the brethren:

²³ And they wrote letters by them after this manner; The apostles and elders and brethren send greeting unto the brethren which are of the Gentiles in Antioch and Syria and Cilicia.

²⁴ Forasmuch as we have heard, that certain which went out from us have troubled you with words, subverting your souls, saying, Ye must be circumcised, and keep the law: to whom we gave no such commandment:

[25] It seemed good unto us, being assembled with one accord, to send chosen men unto you with our beloved Barnabas and Paul,

[26] Men that have hazarded their lives for the name of our Lord Jesus Christ.

[27] We have sent therefore Judas and Silas, who shall also tell you the same things by mouth.

[28] For it seemed good to the Holy Ghost, and to us, to lay upon you no greater burden than these necessary things;

[29] That ye abstain from meats offered to idols, and from blood, and from things strangled, and from fornication: from which if ye keep yourselves, ye shall do well. Fare ye well.

[30] So when they were dismissed, they came to Antioch: and when they had gathered the multitude together, they delivered the epistle:

[31] Which when they had read, they rejoiced for the consolation.

Kingdom Life brings a life of freedom and makes church life a subculture to Kingdom Life.

Galatians 3:28

There is neither Jew nor Greek, there is neither bond nor free, there is neither male nor female: for ye are all one in Christ Jesus.

Colossians 3:11

Where there is neither Greek nor Jew, circumcision nor uncircumcision, Barbarian, Scythian, bond nor free: but Christ is all, and in all.

Paul went on to say:

1 Corinthians 6:9-12 (KJV)

⁹ Know ye not that the unrighteous shall not inherit the kingdom of God? Be not deceived: neither fornicators, nor idolaters, nor adulterers, nor effeminate, nor abusers of themselves with mankind,

¹⁰ Nor thieves, nor covetous, nor drunkards, nor revilers, nor extortioners, shall inherit the kingdom of God.

¹¹ And such were some of you: but ye are washed, but ye are sanctified, but ye are justified in the name of the Lord Jesus, and by the Spirit of our God.

¹² All things are lawful unto me, but all things are not expedient: all things are lawful for me, but I will not be brought under the power of any.

The Kingdom Life message has been consistently contaminated by false declarations that Jesus never spoke nor intended to be spoken. We must be careful to not perpetuate the images and declarations representative of false leaders who have hidden in the midst of those leaders selected by God to transform the world into Jesus' image.

The Book of Jude says this:

³ Beloved, when I gave all diligence to write unto you of the common salvation, it was needful for me to write unto you, and exhort you that ye should earnestly contend for the faith which was once delivered unto the saints.

⁴ For there are certain men crept in unawares, who were before of old ordained to this condemnation, ungodly men, turning the grace of our God into lasciviousness, and denying the only Lord God, and our Lord Jesus Christ.

⁵ I will therefore put you in remembrance, though ye once knew this, how that the Lord, having saved the people out of the land of Egypt, afterward destroyed them that believed not.

Kingdom Life is The Life of God inside you bringing the fullness of the measure and stature of Jesus Christ conforming YOU to HIS image.

In the Kingdom there is no sickness, nor disease. In the Kingdom there is no rich, nor poor. In the Kingdom there is no bond nor free, there is no greater than nor smaller than, no big I nor little you, no loser nor failure, no good nor bad. In the Kingdom everything you need is always provided and available for you. In the Kingdom everything that Jesus has belongs to you. All of Gods gifts and abilities are yours to use right now. Everything God can do you can do Right Now in The Kingdom. The ONLY thing you cannot do is, give YOUR BLOOD TO FORGIVE SIN. ONLY JESUS' blood can do that. Our blood cannot save anyone. In the Kingdom, eternal life is NOW, not after you die. Jesus has given us everything he owns for our use TODAY, not after we die and go to Heaven. You won't need the gifts of the Spirit in Heaven, God Our Father is there. You won't need to be healed in Heaven, God our Father is there. You won't need money in Heaven. The streets are more valuable than money. So why does God speak of riches and health and prosperity and victory and tongues, and love, and miracles, and the power of God, and talents, and resurrection in the Bible? Because those are things we must have ON EARTH as it is IN HEAVEN right now.

In short, EVERTHING Jesus can do we can do right now because of Kingdom Life. You don't have One gift, you have ALL gifts right now in The Kingdom. You are in The Kingdom. The Church has done what the Pharisees and Sadducees did in the Old Testament. The Church has limited the Power of God flowing to His people because of wrong concepts. St John 17:14 tells us, "...We are not of this world because Jesus is not of this world". The same things Jesus did we can do Right Now because of Kingdom Life. So why aren't we doing them? We don't because we think differently about who we are in Christ Jesus.

Gal 4:1-7

1 Now I say, That the heir, as long as he is a child, differeth nothing from a servant, though he be lord of all; ² But is under tutors and governors until the time appointed of the father.³ Even so we, when we were children, were in bondage under the elements of the world: ⁴ But when the fullness of the time was come, God sent forth his Son, made of a woman, made under the law, ⁵ To redeem them that were under the law, that we might receive the adoption of sons. ⁶ And because ye are sons, God hath sent forth the Spirit of his Son into your hearts, crying, Abba, Father. ⁷ Wherefore thou art no more a servant, but a son; and if a son, then an heir of God through Christ.

We must finish the School of the Holy Spirit and accept our diploma in divine living. If we insist that we are ONLY HUMAN, we reject these gifts, talents, abilities and the recognition of God in our lives by saying God is not with me. Greater things shall you do because I go to my Father says Jesus. You will do greater things than I have done when you graduate from the School of the Holy Spirit. All your needs will be supplied according to my riches in glory declares Jesus. Why does he say this? Jesus is King of His Kingdom and God His Father has given him all things for us. We must accept.

> Church life is NOT Kingdom Life because the Church rejects the ability of each saint to become the "measure of the stature of the fullness of Christ"

God created Israel under Abraham's covenant like He established the Church under Jesus' Kingdom Covenant. As the creator, God would need subjects to carry out His plan for the universal community He is establishing. Earth being the beginning project, God has made Jesus the Program manager for all earth holdings. Jesus is the spiritual leader of the Church now and Jesus will become the ruler and King of this earth when he returns. Jesus will fulfill the promise of God in Isa. 9:6-7 which states in part "...and the government shall be upon his shoulders." As

Jesus stated to Peter in Luke 22:25-30, the disciples will judge the 12 tribes of Israel while we manage the rest of the world as the assistants of Christ. ([29] Lk 22:29-30…and I appoint…tribes of Israel. as my Father hath appointed unto me;[30] That ye may eat and drink at my table in my kingdom, and sit on thrones judging the twelve tribes of Israel.)

As the Ekklesia we have to develop the skills needed to manage Jesus' Kingdom on earth. Jesus' earthly throne will replicate his Father's throne in heaven in function, power, and authority.

As Christ's followers we have been promised these positions as stated.

Matthew 19:28

Jesus said to them, "truly I tell you at the renewal of all things, when the Son of Man sits on his glorious throne, you who have followed me will also sit on twelve thrones, judging the twelve tribes of Israel."

Jesus has appointed the five-fold leadership team of the church to train his leaders for these tasks but this training is not being completed by church leaders.

As we come to the end of the age, God our creator is requiring an acceleration in the development of the saints and if need be, He will take over the process Himself. Saints must be prepared to fill Kingdom management needs upon Christ's return. Jesus will have no time to do this while He is ruling and reigning from Jerusalem and the magical transformation most believers think is going to happen by being raptured and given a glorified body I don't think will happen that way. A time of instruction will be needed for certain members of Jesus' Kingdom to run the world as God our Father has declared in Heb 1:13-14, "…until Jesus enemies become His footstool." As a reward to those most note worth, God our Father will retain these saints to rule around His heavenly throne (Rev 3:12). According to Joel 2:1-11 the army of Christ will be unbeatable. After a thousand years, God our Creator will move His Heavenly Kingdom to the same location as earth and call it the New Jerusalem. From here God will begin his expansion and transformation of the universe into His image and likeness (Rev 21:22-27; 22:1-11).

CHAPTER 6

ANCIENT KINGDOMS

Daniel 7:13-18, 21-22

" I was watching in the night visions, And behold, One like the Son of Man, Coming with the clouds of heaven! He came to the Ancient of Days, And they brought Him near before Him. Then to Him was given dominion and glory and a kingdom, That all peoples, nations, and languages should serve Him. His dominion is an everlasting dominion, Which shall not pass away, And His kingdom the one Which shall not be destroyed. "I, Daniel, was grieved in my spirit [a]within my body, and the visions of my head troubled me. I came near to one of those who stood by, and asked him the truth of all this. So he told me and made known to me the interpretation of these things: 'Those great beasts, which are four, are four kings which arise out of the earth. But the saints of the Most High shall receive the kingdom, and possess the kingdom forever, even forever and ever.' "I was watching; and the same horn was making war against the saints, and prevailing against them, until the Ancient of Days came, and a judgment was made in favor of the saints of the Most High, and the time came for the saints to possess the kingdom.

Kingdom Life is not demonstrated by any one nation as it pertains to living in Jesus Kingdom. Among the nations of the world there is a common misconception that Christianity started in America. The world has seen America trumpet the Gospel so strongly that it declares as a defacto truth America started Christianity. The truth is that Jews who believed in the Messiah started Christianity from Israel. Yes, that little tiny nation everyone wants to fight over is the birth place of The Gospel of Jesus Christ and we get to share in the blessing of worldwide salvation. Kingdom Life is the ability to embrace the principles, standards, concepts, and culture of Jesus' Kingdom daily. The Gospel message is meant for ALL peoples of the world, not just some people. God eliminated the distinctions between people after Jesus was raised from the dead. After this event, God no longer separated the world by race, creed, or color but by the identification of saved or unsaved among the human race and those who are for Jesus or against Jesus. The Gospel as read in John 3:16-20 tells the story of God's heart and the acceptance or rejection of Salvation that Jesus makes available. Animals and other beings do not qualify for a relationship with God. The Gospel is owned by Jesus himself and not by any nation. However, if there were a nation that has embraced God's established Word as true and necessary, America would be that nation and Israel would be the people God recognizes. We boldly declare the life, death, burial, and resurrection of Jesus to a lost and dying world.

As such, ALL nations have a right to the Gospel of Jesus Christ as their center piece for life. The Bible calls on all nations to accept Jesus as their ONLY leader and His Kingdom Life principles as their life's direction. The Bible says the nation who's God is the Lord shall prosper (Ps 33:12).

In this context, we can see that Kingdom Life is not a copulation of tribal rituals, nor social norms humanity would display as affirmation for living a good life on planet earth. All peoples everywhere are required to submit themselves to the leadership, social structure and ideology of the Bible to declare God's way of living. As such, we become a separate group of God-beings living in plain sight, designated to express and prepare a place for Jesus Christ to establish His Kingdom on Earth in fulfillment of The Lord's Prayer. Additionally we work to establish a God-like environment that will become the dwelling place of Jesus' Kingdom.

Jesus already stated to Pilate that "I have a Kingdom…" (Jn 18:36-37) and God the Father designated that Jesus must reign until "His enemies are made His footstool" (Heb 1:13). So what kind of mindset do we need to have in this life.

This means that NO SINGLE NATION is designated The Kingdom. All nations are to embrace Kingdom Life purposes and activity. To this end, Jesus instructed his disciples to, "Go therefore and make disciples of all the nations…(Mt 28:18-20)" Making Disciples of the nations which will fulfill this "great commission" as we call it. How do you do that? First we send trained representatives of The Kingdom to invite the people of every nation to believe in Jesus Christ as God's Son, who was sacrificed for our sins/wrongs on the cross of Calvary. Those who hear and accept this then learn to believe that Jesus was raised from the dead by His Father, and that He is seated on the Father's right hand in heaven. Once a commitment is made to this Jesus, we begin to live like Jesus directs us to live through learning the Biblical truths expressed in the Holy Bible. As each individual grows and develops a relationship with Jesus we start to influence our nation to embrace Jesus as Savior and the Gospel message continues to spread.

At this juncture, tribal expectation and national traditions are not enforced as Jesus becomes the primary director of how life is lived. Family habits and personal habits become Jesus habits and we conform to Jesus image as the most important way to live. We learn to ask God our Creator for understanding and direction for life's requirements instead of following the usual habits of our neighbors, friends, family or society. We embrace God's ways as OUR ways and seek for greater understanding and knowledge of how to do things God's way through prayer and studying the Bible and the leadership of the Holy Spirit. We know that Jesus' Kingdom doctrines are the doctrines we must live in order to be just like him, so I am willing to remove ALL THINGS that stop me from becoming just like Jesus in <u>all</u> areas of my life. This includes business, family relations, and spiritual activities. We understand that the way Jesus lives is NOT the way the world lives and we make sure we eliminate all areas of conflict in favor of Jesus' ways and ideas. We are no longer bound to the earth, we are only bound to Kingdom principles.

The Kingdom described in Zechariah 14 will begin on earth after the rapture or catching away of the saints as described in 1 Thes 4:13-18. Those who died believing in Jesus Christ will come alive again and be given a new glorified body that can never die. Then we will serve Jesus as King of His Earthly Kingdom for 1000 years. During this time many miraculous advances in earth life will take place. Eventually another war will break out and the earth will be destroyed after Jesus and God His Father remove all people who lived for Jesus on earth. At that time all people will be changed into people fully developed into the image of Jesus and live with God forever (1 Cor 15:ALL).

GOD DOES NOT TREAT NATIONS LIKE MANKIND TREATS THE NATIONS

CHAPTER 7

HOW DOES KINGDOM LIFE WORK?

Matthew 6:33

In Jesus' Kingdom miracles are not needed because nothing ever breaks

In the Kingdom Jesus is King everyday and <u>Jesus runs the day-to-day activities</u> not the five-fold ministers. In the Kingdom everyone is in agreement on how things are done. In The Kingdom everybody has the same gifts in number and ability. In The Kingdom resurrection life is active right now for everyone. In The Kingdom there is only one (1) death experience and that happens before the RT (Resurrection Translation) takes place as a part of your born again experience. In The Kingdom, you have access to everything Jesus knows. In The Kingdom only truth is spoken. There are no innuendos. ALL Speech is plain. In The Kingdom Angelic action is a daily Visible activity.

Kingdom Life is managed by Jesus alone as King and all assignments are accepted without feedback or alteration in actions. No adjustments are needed because Jesus gives the directions clearly and without ambiguity.

Any suggestion from me is a violation of protocol. No sickness, disease, infirmity, or illness exists in the Kingdom. Kingdom life is non-violent because there is no power other than Jesus' power and authority. In Kingdom Life there is unity, love and peace ALL the time. My excellent skills do not lessen the skills or intelligence or strength of my fellow brother or sister. There is NO COMPETITION in the Kingdom. In fact, competition is forbidden. All ideas and new works come from Jesus. There are NO LOSERS, everybody wins ALL the time. Life is harmonious and communication is always understood no matter what the topic because self is eliminated in the Kingdom. You are no more important than I.

The focus of Kingdom Life is not to acquire stuff, but to complete the mission of establishing the Kingdom to Earth as it is in heaven. Once this is complete, the mission is to make Jesus King of All peoples and All lands everywhere on earth. All governments will submit to Kingdom Management and All earthly leaders will submit to Jesus as King OVER them (please read Zechariah 14:ALL). We will not be centered in one location, but manage everyplace on earth ALL the time. We will voluntarily complete all actions according to what needs to be done to completely establish Jesus' Kingdom on earth. The Kingdom is both futuristic and current.

Jesus' Kingdom is NOT the Kingdom of God the Father. Jesus' Kingdom is NOT heaven, but it functions under the exact requirements of heaven just like the Father's Throne.

Lk 22:28-30 says, [28] "But you are those who have continued with Me in My trials. [29] And I bestow upon you a kingdom, just as My Father bestowed one upon Me, [30] that you may eat and drink at My table in My kingdom, and sit on thrones judging the twelve tribes of Israel."

Jesus had already promised Kingdom benefits to his disciples and this mother wanted to make sure her boys were the first in line for the best positions available. The other disciples saw that they were trying to "skip the line" so to speak and became upset. Clearly we understand that Jesus is talking about His Kingdom, not the Father's heaven. We can also see that this is a case of dual citizenship with earthly manifestations carried out while the disciples prepared the Church on earth.

Mt 20:20-25 makes the same statements from a different angle: [20] Then the mother of Zebedee's sons came to Him with her sons, kneeling down and asking something from Him.[21] And He said to her, "What do you wish?" She said to Him, "Grant that these two sons of mine may sit, one on Your right hand and the other on the left, in Your kingdom."[22] But Jesus answered and said, "You do not know what you ask. Are you able to drink the cup that I am about to drink, [a]and be baptized with the baptism that I am baptized with?" They said to Him, "We are able."[23] So He said to them, "You will indeed drink My cup, [b] and be baptized with the baptism that I am baptized with; but to sit on My right hand and on My left is not Mine to give, but it is for those for whom it is prepared by My Father."

This same conversation takes place again in Mk 10:35-44 as a comparative verse. While Jesus' mandate is to establish the physical earthly Kingdom in order to place the prophesied Kingdom of Isaiah 9:6-7 into operational status, our mandate is to learn the mental, academic, inter-relational protocols and functions of the Kingdom right now. This way we can properly relate to Jesus as King of His Kingdom. Because we are members of the human species we have the right to start these changes in earth today!

This truth transfers Jesus' Kingdom to earth right now. More scriptural rederences on this point are Mt 16:28; Mt 20:21; Mt 25:34; Lk 22:30; Lk 23:42 just to mention a few. We are mandated to make the earth as it is in heaven today, not after we die. As such, Jesus gave us the five-fold ministry as an instrument of training to become Kingdom citizens.

Adonia, Elohim, Yaweh, God our Father, always intended for us, as the human race, to inter-relate with him in this Kingdom manner after we are born again. These abilities ensure a direct link to God's will, plan, and purpose on a 24 hour 7 day a week basis. Having to pray through because of competing mental processes was not in the picture as God communicated His direction for our lives. However, communications became a struggle because of original sin. For those who have seen the movies Terminator with Arnold Schwarzenegger, or Star Trek battling the Borg Nation, this is a similar system of communications to God's way of communicating. In those fictitious cultures, no words are needed to communicate directions. When you just think it, everyone knows what you are thinking. The process of metamorphosis allows us to work the same way on earth as in heaven by allowing the Spirit to complete metamorphosis within us. Additionally, there is no feedback by the team to the directions of King Jesus since there is NEVER a disagreement with what needs to be done (Jn 5:16-30). In Jesus' Kingdom, nobody ever has a better idea.

As humans in transformation, we have a long way to go in this area. We think it is our right to introduce an alternative method of activity to validate our worth or improve the product. Our verbiage does not validate us in Jesus Kingdom, but our <u>direct obedience does</u>. Jesus is the King and He alone directs Kingdom activity. No one else but Jesus and at this point, not even The Father injects instructions. The plan was given "at the foundation of the world". Please read John 5:19-27 for clarification.

<u>Mt 25:34</u>

Then shall the King say unto them on his right hand, Come, ye blessed of my Father, inherit the kingdom prepared for you from the foundation of the world:

Since salvation, our need as Kingdom Citizens, is to learn the standards, communications skills, and values of The King. We then implement those attributes into our daily lives for functionality. Romans 12:2-3 calls this Transformation. No longer are we Earth Citizens, but Kingdom Citizens and we are "expected" to act like, talk like, think like, and walk like Jesus does as King of His Kingdom while we are on earth. You say, I have not seen anybody do this. Well, then YOU become the first, just like Jesus was the first man born from the dead. These actions must not be put off or delayed until "After Death". If we take that attitude, Jesus' Kingdom will not be established. Acts 3: 20-21 says, "and He shall send Jesus Christ, which before was preached unto you: Whom the heaven must receive until the times of restitution of all things, which God hath spoken by the mouth of His holy prophets since the world began." The potential would be for Jesus to have no place to reside when he returns. If John the Baptist had the attitude some Christians maintain today, Jesus would have never made it to the Cross of Calvary. Jesus at least needs the Mount of Olives to place his feet upon. Kingdom Life and The Kingdom of God is a multifaceted event and a current reality!

Thinking about some of the statements Jesus made while preaching on earth, How could the Pharisees shut the doors of the Kingdom when Jesus had not been crucified? Mt 23:13, "Woe to you, teachers of the law and Pharisees, you hypocrites! You shut the door of the kingdom of heaven in people's faces. You yourselves do not enter, nor will you let those enter who are trying to." What a statement! Was Kingdom Life available before Jesus died on the cross?

<u>Kingdom Life is the replacement for earth life</u>

Kingdom Life is not an <u>add-on</u> to earth life. Kingdom Life is the replacement for earth life, just like it is a replacement for Human life, church life, social, tribal, and cultural life. At this point the statement of Isaiah 55:8 is not relevant because our ways must become God's ways or we are not living Kingdom Life. Our metamorphosis must begin to form visible physical, mental, and active definition in order to validate our connection to Jesus' Kingdom. If you don't look like or talk like or walk like Jesus, you are probably NOT like Jesus.

Several scripture come to mind at this point.

1 John 3:1-3 – (KJV)

Behold, what manner of love the Father hath bestowed upon us, that we should be called the sons of God: therefore the world knoweth us not, because it knew him not.

² Beloved, now are we the sons of God, and it doth not yet appear what we shall be: but we know that, when he shall appear, we shall be like him; for we shall see him as he is.

³ And every man that hath this hope in him purifieth himself, even as he is pure.

1 John 3:5-6 – ⁵ And ye know that he was manifested to take away our sins; and in him is no sin. ⁶ Whosoever abideth in him sinneth not: whosoever sinneth hath not seen him, neither known him.

1 John 3:9 - ⁹ Whosoever is born of God doth not commit sin; for his seed remaineth in him: and he cannot sin, because he is born of God.

1 John 4:17 - ¹⁷ Herein is our love made perfect, that we may have boldness in the day of judgment: because as he is, so are we in this world.

St John 17:14, 16 - ¹⁴ I have given them thy word; and the world hath hated them, because they are not of the world, even as I am not of the world. ¹⁶ They are not of the world, even as I am not of the world.

Kingdom Life is not earth life
Kingdom Life is not human life
Kingdom Life is not church life
Kingdom Life is not social or tribal or cultural life
Kingdom Life is not American life

Kingdom Life transforms the believer into the fullness of the measure and stature of Jesus Christ conforming us to HIS image.

Jesus exclusively taught about Kingdom Life while on earth. The Apostles, called by Jesus to be disciples, were not told how to live earth life, they were told how to live Kingdom Life. The people were astounded by Jesus' teaching because He was telling them how things functioned in His Kingdom and these actions were tremendously different than life on earth. So much so that even the guards for the Sanhedrin said, "… Never a man spoke like this man…" (Jn 7:44-47) Kingdom Life can be lived on earth, but Kingdom Life is NOT earth life and everybody knew this who heard Jesus.

As Christians in today's world, we think that we can live an earth life and be accepted in the Kingdom realm. We expect Jesus to perform miracles, signs and wonders on our behalf. However, miracles do not come from earth, they come from The Kingdom alone. You cannot get a miracle from the earth. Miracles have to come from The Kingdom. You want to live an earth life, then do not expect Kingdom advantages. NO. To gain Kingdom access, you have to make the transition of Transformation which REQUIRES metamorphosis. This is a permanent change in ALL areas of life one step at a time. Jesus was not transfigured by accident on the Mount of Transfiguration. He positioned himself so that God, His

Father could do those things while he was still On Earth, proving to us that WE can do these things on earth also.

CHAPTER 8

THE COVENANT IS NOW THE PROMISE

In the spring of 2018 I made my first missions trip to Africa. I was excited and blown away with the cultural continuation of tribal norms and mores. Everywhere you looked you could see how the ancient social, political and tribal activities continued to inhabit the mindsets of the people and nation. Being an African meant you had to have a tribe and you had to belong to a nation within the African continent to have legitimacy among the people. Otherwise you were a foreigner and seen as such. You were a person from the outside, maybe a nice person from the outside, but none the less a person from the outside. It did not matter what you possessed or how much you possessed, you were from the outside and EVERYONE understood this. You would always be second, not first in the activity of the community, but as a guest you have dignity and respect and protection for the period of time you are there.

Kingdom Life has a distribution of provision and opportunities attached to it much like this process in Africa. Those "in the family" are prioritized for distribution of goods and services that are exclusive to "The Kingdom".

God gave Moses, as the Law Giver, a substitute or bypass plan for the Blood Covenant of Abraham. Because the Israelites had violated the Abrahamic Covenant, the Law was added as a substitute condition to the Blood Covenant until the Promised Seed should come (Gal 3:19). After Jesus was crucified and Resurrected from the dead, God destroyed the Law making a BETTER COVENANT as He brought in the Gentiles to the family of God creating the Church.

The Law was NOT THE SAME as the Covenant God made with Abraham. The Law was The Law of Moses and NOT The Covenant of Abraham. The original preference and controlling emphasis for God was for the Blood Covenant of Abraham to remain. But after Jesus resurrection the Law was discontinued and the Abrahamic Covenant was altered to come in agreement with Jesus Blood Covenant. So once the purpose for The Law was completed, i.e....the sacrifice of Jesus on the Cross of Calvary, The Law is discontinued in its entirety. Jesus grandfathered in certain truths and actions of The Covenant, including the 10 Commandments to allow for Temple Worship to restart at the appropriate time. Control of The Kingdom is given to Jesus as the New Blood Covenant takes control after his resurrection. (Dan 7:13-14) Kingdom Life is now under the full authority of Jesus Blood Covenant. The devil has no legal authority concerning compliance concerning the operation of Jesus Kingdom. As a result, both Jew and Gentile can now be saved.

In the book of Acts the new rules for Gentile Salvation are applied:

Chapter 15, "22 Then pleased it the apostles and elders with the whole church, to send chosen men of their own company to Antioch with Paul and Barnabas; namely, Judas surnamed Barnabas and Silas, chief men among the brethren: 23 And they wrote letters by them after this manner; The apostles and elders and brethren send greeting unto the brethren which are of the Gentiles in Antioch and Syria and Cilicia. 24 Forasmuch as we have heard, that certain which went out from us have troubled you with words, subverting your souls, saying, Ye must be circumcised, and keep the law: to whom we gave no such commandment: [25] It seemed good unto us, being assembled with one accord, to send chosen men unto you with our beloved Barnabas and Paul, [26] Men that have hazarded their lives for the name of our Lord Jesus Christ. [27] We have sent therefore Judas and Silas, who shall also tell you the same things by mouth. [28] For it seemed good to the Holy Ghost, and to us, to lay upon you no greater burden than these necessary things; [29] That ye abstain from meats offered to idols, and from blood, and from things strangled, and from fornication: from which if ye keep yourselves, ye shall do well. Fare ye well."

Kingdom Life overrules earth life. Kingdom Life suspends the rules of physics and resistance and economics because Kingdom Life removes the barriers that limit productive and creative activity while establishing limitations only on those things that violate God's supernatural structure. Whatever is good and kind and holy, worthy of honor, and lovely and just now rules the day. (Phil 4:8)

In the Kingdom there is no hate, nor sin because the King rules the Kingdom and the most important rule is Love. Jesus' Blood Sacrifice destroyed ALL SIN FOREVER in The Kingdom. Therefore SIN does NOT exist in the Kingdom. On earth sin still exists because Satan is still the god of the earth, but we must make a choice. Are you a citizen of The Kingdom or are you a citizen of the earth? In the Kingdom there is no inequality; in the Kingdom everything that God is, is available to you and inside you (Jn 14:17-23; Jn 17:14-29). In the Kingdom there is no black nor white, no color nor nationality, there is no young nor old, there is no rich nor poor in the Kingdom. In the Kingdom everyone is a Son of God because there are no sexes in The Kingdom and there is no marriage (Mt 22:30) Therefore everything Jesus can do, YOU can do also. ALL the ABILITIES of GOD are yours. In The Kingdom the Church as we know it does not exist, only member saints who are Sons of God because Jesus is the ONLY King and leader. (1 Cor 15:20-28) In The Kingdom everyone is anointed all the time. In The Kingdom there are unlimited positions for activity and production.

In The Kingdom there is only ONE ruler. In The Kingdom ALL gifts, talents, and abilities are ACTIVE ALL the time in EVERYBODY. Like Jesus said, "you are in the world, but not OF the world…" Kingdom Life is all about becoming Just Like Jesus. Everything else is secondary to your transformation into a Complete Son of God. Galatians says it this way,

Gal 3:23-29, Ch 4:1-7

²³ But before faith came, we were kept under the law, shut up unto the faith which should afterwards be revealed. ²⁴ Wherefore the law was our schoolmaster to bring us unto Christ, that we might be justified by faith. ²⁵ But after that faith is come, we are no longer under a schoolmaster. ²⁶ For ye are all the children of God by faith in Christ Jesus. ²⁷ For as many of you as have been baptized into Christ have put on Christ. ²⁸ There is neither Jew nor Greek, there is neither bond nor free, there is neither male nor female: for ye are all one in Christ Jesus. ²⁹ And if ye be Christ's, then are ye Abraham's seed, and heirs according to the promise.

4 Now I say, That the heir, as long as he is a child, differeth nothing from a servant, though he be lord of all; ² But is under tutors and governors until the time appointed of the father. ³ Even so we, when we were children, were in bondage under the elements of the world: ⁴ But when the fullness of the time was come, God sent forth his Son, made of a woman, made under the law, ⁵ To redeem them that were under the law, that we might receive the adoption of sons. ⁶ And because ye are sons, God hath sent forth the Spirit of his Son into your hearts, crying, Abba, Father. ⁷ Wherefore thou art no more a servant, but a son; and if a son, then an heir of God through Christ.

Abraham learned how the covenant made his relationship with God our Father a priority. This priority is related to everything God would do on planet earth.

In Gen 18:16-33, God, himself is visiting Abraham as he travels to Sodom and Gomorrah because God has a serious issue to resolve and serious actions to take. God is about to destroy several thousand human souls and He is going to give the final vote to Abraham because Abraham is a Covenant Man. God made this agreement (Covenant) with Abraham that requires God to make no decision without Abraham's approval on matters concerning the earth. In this case, Abraham's nephew, Lot, lives in a city that God is wanting to destroy because the sin of homosexuality has become the primary way of life. These citizens would demand that Lot, Abraham's nephew, release the visiting Angels at Lot's home to come outside and have sex with them as some kind of initiation or ritual within the city.

Scripture says in Gen 18:17-23, that God our Father talks to himself about this decision and comes to the conclusion that He will discuss His idea with Abraham before finalizing His actions against Sodom and Gomorrah. Listen to God's thinking about His relationship with Abraham and the critical value he puts on Abraham's agreement (Covenant) before He acts:

Gen 18:17-23

[17] And the LORD said, "Shall I hide from Abraham what I am doing, [18] since Abraham shall surely become a great and mighty nation, and all the nations of the earth shall be blessed in him? [19] For I have known him, in order that he may command his children and his household after him, that they keep the way of the LORD, to do righteousness and justice, that the LORD may bring to Abraham what He has spoken to him." [20] And the LORD said, "Because the outcry against Sodom and Gomorrah is great, and because their sin is very grave, [21] I will go down now and see whether they have done altogether according to the outcry against it that has come to Me; and if not, I will know."

[22] Then the men turned away from there and went toward Sodom, but Abraham still stood before the LORD. [23] And Abraham came near and said, "Would You also destroy the righteous with the wicked?

Look at how carefully God the Creator ponders his decision because of His relationship with Abraham. Look at the way God changes things to satisfy Abraham's concerns. The Creator of the Universe is waiting to finalize His choice until after He has had a conversation with His man on earth (Kingdom) because this man is a Covenant Man.

We have a Covenant with Jesus Christ and God is waiting to finalize every action He takes in your life with YOU because you are a Covenant Man with Jesus. Yet how serious is this truth in our lives? How many times have we violated the Covenant? We have not recognized God's appearances in our lives nor do we hear His voice speaking to us.

Important matters await our conversation with the Lord. (Jn 10:1-5) This is the way The Kingdom works for us today. "Today, if you will hear his voice, harden not your heart..." (Heb 4:7).

As Kingdom citizens we are afforded opportunities that earth citizens cannot have unless they receive Jesus as their savior. We have special favor over everyone else. Because of Jesus' Blood Covenant, God the Father treats us differently than every other person on planet earth. God gives the Covenant Man the special tool of Prayer to communicate with Himself. This prayer of desperation creates a special conversation as described in Rom 8:26-27 and Eph 6: 18. In prayer we communicate the intricate details we need for God's intervention and God communicates his plans for earth. I believe these are times when God will instruct us on what to pray. Our speech, while speaking in tongues, also dictates our needs to God while God is telling us how to come in agreement with the plans He has already set in motion. God calls us Son and gives us a seat at His table of power, authority, and blessing. God needs us to intercede for His plans to succeed in the earth against His enemy, the devil.

If you don't have Jesus as your savior and you want to be a part of this great army of believers, you can request salvation right now.

Repeat this statement: A Prayer For Salvation

Repeat this Prayer after me:

Lord Jesus I come to you confessing that I am a sinner. I recognize and acknowledge that you are The Son of God and that you died for my sins. I ask you to forgive me my sins and wash me in your Blood from every sin I have committed. According to Romans 10:9-10 I confess with my mouth that Jesus Is Lord, and I believe in my heart that God the Father raised Him from the dead and therefore I am saved. Father God, you said that if any man come to you, you will not cast him out. I thank you Father God that you have accepted me into your family and I am saved by the Blood and name of Jesus. I also ask the Holy Spirit to Baptize me in His Power with the evidence of speaking in other tongues. Thank you Lord God that I am Saved.

Continue:

Mr. Devil. I renounce any agreements or commitments I have made with you in my life. I cancel every agreement and contract I ever made and I give back all goods and possessions that I received as a result of these agreements and contracts in what ever form they came. I decree that I belong to Jesus Christ of Nazareth, The Son of The God of Creation and I will never serve you again!!!!

Declare:

Now Father God, I ask you to activate every gift, talent, or calling in my life and I decree and declare that your purpose for my life is established this day. I agree for your will to be done in my life and your kingdom to come in my life from this day forward. I terminate every assignment of hell sent to destroy and derail your plans and purposes for me and my family from this day forward.

Decree:

I decree that I Serve Jesus and I will not serve another from this day forward. I declare that the Blood of Jesus destroyed the works of the Devil against me and there is nothing that will ever hurt me again because of Jesus' Blood. I am saved and I belong to Jesus and I will never belong to the devil again. I speak and state that my life is in Christ, Hidden in his blood and every curse is cancelled against me. I am a Son or Daughter of God and He has accepted me into His family. I'm Saved, I'm Saved, I'm Saved. Hallelujah!!! Thank You Lord!

****

Jesus, as the Son of God I believe you died on the cross for my sins. I ask you to wash me in your blood and forgive me my sins right now. Father God, your word says that any man who comes to you, you will not cast him aside. Thank you for accepting me into your family as a son the way you have accepted Jesus. Holy Spirit, I accept you as my teacher, anointer, and leader. Speak The Word of God into my ear every day. Baptize me now in your power so I can be a witness for Jesus my savior all my life. Thank you Lord Jesus for saving me, In Jesus name amen.

CHAPTER 9

ENTERING THE KINGDOM

You have just made a decision to receive Jesus as your personal Lord and Savior. Here are a few things you need to know.

Your Identity has changed. You are no longer XYZ, you are now a Son of the Living God, the creator of the Universe and a brother to Jesus Christ your savior. You are a Kingdom citizen and a member of the Ekklesia - The Church of Jesus Christ. You are the same as Christ to every believer and especially to the devil and his demons.

This Kingdom message of salvation, has declared Jesus is Lord of your life. As such you have all power in heaven and earth to conduct your business without being hindered by satan and you are free from harassment by the devils minions. Your power and authority comes from God the Father and the Blood of Jesus Christ who destroyed the works of the devil after being raised from the dead by the power of God the Father. (Acts 13:30)

Reality causes us to pray for many different reasons and in many different ways. But even with our pressing needs in life, God needs us to pray for the things that will bring Jesus back to earth. I call these prayers Kingdom prayers. While these prayers are not prayers to solve my individual needs in life, they are prayers designed to return Jesus to the earth. This is much like John the Baptist preparing the world for Jesus' first coming, in like manner we also partnership with God the Father to complete His plan for Jesus return to His Kingdom. Our petitions have the ability to bring into existence the events, outcomes, and activities that establish Jesus as King in the earth today. These prayers are designed to lead us into the 22rd century with Jesus as the Lord of Lords and King of Kings. The world and humanity will be a better place and then become the utopia God our Creator has declared it should be.

For this purpose these prayers are devoid of selfish need or greed because they embody the full expectations of God for Christ's rulership and dominion in this place called earth. Like the master who went away to receive his kingdom, Jesus will return to set up a sin-free society for all mankind. During this time, even babies could live to be 1000 years old. These prayers are designed to create God's pattern and method of life everywhere. As we pray Jesus will become the overseer of all the earth. Nothing will remain untouched by His hands. Earth as we know it becomes transformed into the essence of the Garden of Eden before Adam sinned. We have been bought with a price, we are not our own(1 Cor 6:18-20; 7:23). We serve God as Jesus positions Christianity to be the final and dominant lifestyle for the world. Jesus will declare, "Thy Kingdom has Come Thy Will is Being Done On Earth as it is in Heaven" to the glory of God the Father.

Kingdom prayers also focus on transforming us into the exact image of Christ. Truly we have needs that must be met, but our greatest need is to become just like Jesus. In order to do that we must get a better understanding of who Jesus really is. Our current profile is lacking in too many ways. Many have made Jesus a teddy bear love giver who rescues everybody from every wrong and evil or He is a guy who just wants to kill you and get it over with. So many Christians are just simply hoping that we would die first and be done with the hassle of change. What if that ideology is insufficient for us to be caught up when the trumpet call is made for the resurrection. Not looking enough like Jesus could make the difference.

1 John 3:1-3 says"… Behold, what manner of love the Father hath bestowed upon us, that we should be called the sons of God: therefore the world knoweth us not, because it knew him not. [2] Beloved, now are we the sons of God, and it doth not yet appear what we shall be: but we know that, when he shall appear, we shall be like him; for we shall see him as he is. [3] And every man that hath this hope in him purifieth himself, even as he is pure."

Kingdom prayers focus on my changing into the exact image of Christ (Rom 8:29). As such, am I prepared to become a Kingdom person NOW? Or, am I waiting for Christ to return and finish the job for me. I am not saying that we can make this change on our own, but I am saying that our prayers must be sufficiently different than they are now. They must be bolder, more intense, they must demand that my human boundaries are not boundaries to God. I must not be satisfied with what others say is OK. I must insist that God do something more in my life today greater than yesterday helping me to be just like Him.

Kingdom prayers are not earth prayers although I am born on earth, they are not about humanity. These prayers are not church prayers although I go to church, they are not tribal or cultural, or national prayers either. Yes I love and desire to see my nation do well, I love and desire to see my people flourish, I love and desire to see my culture become the best it can be, but I recognize the flaws in the system make this scenario a losing plan. Jesus is the kind of person who knew that the people were lost and sought to give them a new and better way to live. He gave us the solution to earth life, he gave us the solution to human life and church or synagogue life that mankind could not provide. By doing this Jesus was able to change the world of his day. He was able to impact governments and cultures and move the world to a better place of existence through His obedient life to our Father/creator while He prepared the world to receive His Kingdom rulership. Unfortunately we have not maintained the spiritual pressure necessary to implement Jesus' plan. Here are a few prayers to get you thinking in a way that will support Jesus' Kingdom being established.

PRAYER

Rom 12:2 is a well known scripture by most who believe, "…and be not conformed to this world, but be transformed by the renewing of your mind, that you may prove what is that good and acceptable and perfect will of God."

Few if any of us really believe we can be perfect. Some think you can be good. Maybe a few more believe you can be acceptable to God. Yet God clearly states that we must become these things to HIM. How do you get there? You must pray with the idea I am this to God today! the idea I CAN become this to God today! Mark 11:23-24 says, "… 23 For verily I say unto you, That whosoever shall say unto this mountain, Be thou removed, and be thou cast into the sea; and shall not doubt in his heart, but shall believe that those things which he saith shall come to pass; he shall have whatsoever he saith. 24 Therefore I say unto you, What things soever ye desire, when ye pray, believe that ye receive them, and ye shall have them."

When we pray we must believe that the things we pray will be done now in this life. We must approach God through Jesus with a burning knowing we are everything He says He says we are. This is a unique opportunity with God. He expects us to believe Him in everything He has said. We have agreed to let God change whatever needs to be changed in us. 1 John 5:14-15 states; "14 And this is the confidence that we have in him, that, if we ask any thing according to his will, he heareth us:[15] And if we know that he hear us, whatsoever we ask, we know that we have the petitions that we desired of him."

I must not say NO to God. My NO to God breaks the Blood Covenant of Jesus and opens us up for the devil to attack, challenge, destroy, and remove all the good things God has done. Yes God does the good things, but the devil can undo the good things just as quickly as God did them because I am saying NO to God.

Here are some prayers to use to help us fully embrace Kingdom Life principles and become fully developed in Kingdom living.

Prayer #1 Rom 12:2... [2] And be not conformed to this world: but be ye transformed by the renewing of your mind, that ye may prove what is that good, and acceptable, and perfect, will of God.

<u>Pray</u>
God, cause me to reject the areas where I conform to this world. Change me in a way that I will have the mind of Christ to prove what is that good and acceptable and perfect will of God. I ask you to do this and I believe this can be done, in Jesus' name.

If you pray in tongues, then do that right now for two minutes, not seconds. If you don't pray in tongues, then repeat the statement several times before starting to thank God for doing what He has said he will do. Then shout Hallelujah a couple of times and rejoice!

Prayer #2 Eph 4:13... [13] Till we all come in the unity of the faith, and of the knowledge of the Son of God, unto a perfect man, unto the measure of the stature of the fullness of Christ:

<u>Pray</u>
Father, show me how to have unified faith in your Word! ...But to have UNIFIED faith in Your Word. Lead me to learn the knowledge of Jesus that makes me a perfect man and lead me in the way that will cause me to become the measure and stature of the fullness of Christ, in Jesus' name.

Prayer #3 Eph 4:17-30(ESV)... [17] Now this I say and testify in the Lord, that you must no longer walk as the Gentiles do, in the futility of their minds. [18] They are darkened in their understanding, alienated from the life of God because of the ignorance that is in them, due to their hardness of heart. [19] They have become callous and have given themselves up to sensuality, greedy to practice every kind of impurity. [20] But that is not the way you learned Christ!— [21] assuming that you have heard about him and were taught in him, as the truth is in Jesus, [22] to put off your old self,[a] which belongs to your former manner of life and is corrupt through deceitful desires, [23] and to be renewed in the spirit of your minds, [24] and to put on the new self, created after the likeness of God in true righteousness and holiness. [25] Therefore, having put away falsehood, let each one of you speak the truth with his neighbor, for we are members one of another. [26] Be angry and do not sin; do not let the sun go down on your anger, [27] and give no opportunity to the devil. [28] Let the thief no longer steal, but rather let him labor, doing honest work with his own hands, so that he may have something to share with anyone in need. [29] Let no corrupting talk come out of your mouths, but only such as is good for building up, as fits the occasion, that it may give grace to those who hear. [30] And do not grieve the Holy Spirit of God, by whom you were sealed for the day of redemption.

Pray

Oh God, In Jesus' name, teach me how to give up all my negative behaviors! Teach me how to reject the unclean, greedy, and immoral actions! Father, give me the desire to become everything that pleases you every day. Give me the courage to change what I am doing into what you are doing today. Give me a love for your ways and the power to refuse these temptations in my life. Help my anger submit to the authority of Jesus character and cause me to deny the devil any place in my mind, body, or emotions! I desperately want to be just like Jesus. Let the words of my mouth and the meditation of my heart be acceptable in your sight each day of this process. Make me a greater vessel in your

Kingdom Father. I don't know how to do all these things, but I am ready to learn and change my ways to fit your ways today. In Jesus' name.

Prayer #4 1 Cor 2:9... [9] But as it is written, Eye hath not seen, nor ear heard, neither have entered into the heart of man, the things which God hath prepared for them that love him.

<u>Pray</u>
Lord Sabaoth (Rom 9:29; James 5:4), God of the Angel Armies, grant me the eyes to see as you see and let me see what I have not seen, give me the ear to hear and let me hear what you hear, and give me a heart to feel and respond like you would respond in my life so I can respond like you. Raise my expectations so I can become like you! Change my perspectives that do not reflect you. Cause me to shift my life to prepare for you to take a greater part of me and cause me to operate in your methods each day. In Jesus' name amen.

Kingdom prayers cause me to become a Kingdom citizen in life and spirit, soul and body which completes the whole man of God in the world. I become the replication of Jesus on earth and I convert every place my foot steps as Kingdom property right now. (Josh 1:3)

As long as we live, the Kingdom lives in the earth and we have the authority to change our environment to look just like heaven. Yes we have a long way to go, but we complete the mandate, "thy kingdom come, thy will be done on earth as it is in heaven." We don't have to wait for Jesus to return. We can do this right now!

Our prayers don't <u>just change us</u>, they change the world and cause the world to become The Kingdom of Jesus Christ right now. You and I together praying and demonstrating the actions of Jesus, the thoughts of Jesus, the ways of Jesus become Jesus in the earth. The Pharisee and Sadducee could not stop Christ Jesus in His day. They will not stop us in our day!

Prayer #5 Eph 5:1-15(ESV)... "5 Therefore be imitators of God, as beloved children. ²And walk in love, as Christ loved us and gave himself up for us, a fragrant offering and sacrifice to God. ³But sexual immorality and all impurity or covetousness must not even be named among you, as is proper among saints. ⁴Let there be no filthiness nor foolish talk nor crude joking, which are out of place, but instead let there be thanksgiving. ⁵For you may be sure of this, that everyone who is sexually immoral or impure, or who is covetous (that is, an idolater), has no inheritance in the kingdom of Christ and God. ⁶Let no one deceive you with empty words, for because of these things the wrath of God comes upon the sons of disobedience. ⁷Therefore do not become partners with them; ⁸for at one time you were darkness, but now you are light in the Lord. Walk as children of light ⁹(for the fruit of light is found in all that is good and right and true), ¹⁰and try to discern what is pleasing to the Lord. ¹¹Take no part in the unfruitful works of darkness, but instead expose them. ¹²For it is shameful even to speak of the things that they do in secret. ¹³But when anything is exposed by the light, it becomes visible, ¹⁴for anything that becomes visible is light. Therefore it says,

"Awake, O sleeper,
 and arise from the dead,
and Christ will shine on you."

¹⁵Look carefully then how you walk, not as unwise but as wise,

Pray

Father God, make me sensitive to these types of actions that will compromise my commitment, faith, and morality with you! I am sorry if I have demonstrated any of these unworthy behaviors in your sight and I ask your forgiveness. It is not about people, it is all about me. Forgive me and enable me to overcome these challenges SO I present Jesus in His purest form to the world. I want to be just like Him! Give me the will to cast off the darkness, the anger, the shame, the rebellion, the greed, the hate, that has caused me to miss the mark Christ has set. Show me how to become the fullness of the measure and stature of Christ in this life, so in the life to come I will be able to hear you say, "well done my good and faithful servant." Thank you Father, in Jesus' name.

Prayer #6 Rom 12:3, "[3] For I say, through the grace given unto me, to every man that is among you, not to think of himself more highly than he ought to think; but to think soberly, according as God hath dealt to every man the measure of faith.

Pray

Father show me your ways Lord, so that I will be able to do your acts. Cause me to hunger after you and the ideas you give more than I think of the world and their ideas. Change me into a Kingdom minded person, remove the selfish and emotional manipulation of my heart that have caused me to miss the mark of Christ. Open my eyes to see, my ears to hear, my heart to understand and so that I agree with you every day. I want to become just like Jesus. Give me a covenant mind in Jesus' name, amen.

These are not the only prayers we should be praying. We are certainly learning that Jesus live and taught exclusively on the subject of Kingdom. Following His footsteps is critical for success and the most productive action we can take. These prayers will serve to strengthen our relationship with Christ. Let us always end our prayer the way Jesus taught us.

THY KINGDOM COME, THY WILL BE DONE ON EARTH AS IT IS IN HEAVEN. AMEN!

WORKS CITED

Jewish Virtual Library.org/timeline

Wikipedia.org/wiki/Roman Emperors

www.historyworld.net/historyofthepapacy

Early ChristianWritings.com/1clement.html

www.Britannica.com/event/first-Council-of-Nicaea-325

youtube.com/Yalecourses/PaulFreedman/constantineandtheearlychurch
/lechure series/1-9

Monroe. Miles	2004	Rediscovering The Kingdom
Destiny Image	Shippensburg, PA	
Monroe. Miles	2006	Kingdom Principles
Destiny Image		Shippensburg, PA
Robertson. Pat 1992		The Secret Kingdom
Word Publishing	Dallas, TX	
Schroll. R.C.	2018	History of the Catholic Churc
Legonier Ministries		
Bishop Bill Hamon	1997	Apostles, Prophets, and the Coming
Moves of God		
Destiny Image	Shippensburg, PA	

AUTHOR'S BIOGRAPHY

Luther (Bro Luke) Armstrong completed a career with the US Air Force that spanned 23 years. He is a Prophet to the Nations and has recently returned from East Africa conducting pastor's conferences, church meetings and Bible school seminars in Kenya and Tanzania. His popular message, Kingdom Life, has inspired many. He is an author and member of Christian International Ministries of Santa Rosa Beach, Florida. He has ministered in countries such as Germany, England, Turkey, and Greece giving biblical tours of sites such as Philippi, Thessalonica, and Athens while supporting missionary efforts and helping establish church plants. His training and equipping was pioneered through the International Gospel Outreach Missions Program. His experience will enrich your Spirit and soul and give you a greater desire to answer the call and work of Jesus Christ in your life.

www.ingramcontent.com/pod-product-compliance
Lightning Source LLC
Chambersburg PA
CBHW050857150626
46549CB00013B/2750